LOVE, LIES & CONSEQUENCES

CASSANDRA CARTER

Love, Lies, and Consequences

ISBN: 1495937879
ISBN-13: 978-1495937873

Copyright © 2014 Cassandra Carter

All rights reserved. The reproduction, transmission or utilization of this work in whole or in part in any form by any electronic, mechanical or other means, now known or hereafter invented including xerography, photocopying, and recording, or in any information storage or retrieval system is forbidden without written permission by the author.

This is a work of fiction. Names, characters, places and incidents are either the product of the author's imagination or are used factiously, and any resemblance to actual persons, living or dead, business establishments, events or locales is entirely coincidental.

To everyone who has encouraged me along my writing journey. Thank you for providing me with such inspiration and motivation. Your support is deeply appreciated!

CHAPTER 1

"A tropical storm warning has been issued for the Turks and Caicos and all surrounding areas. This warning remains in effect until 2 AM Eastern Standard Time."

Kyra listened to the recording as satellite images of red and orange traveled across the TV screen. White clouds swirled over a map of the West Indies before moving toward The Gulf as predicted.

"At 4:00 PM the center of tropical storm Anya was located about 240 miles east of the Dominican Republic, moving North-West at about 25 MPH, sustaining maximum winds near 45 MPH, with gusts reaching up to 65 MPH. At this speed, Anya is expected to make landfall late tonight or early tomorrow morning."

Kyra glanced out the window expecting gray clouds however, the sun set the sky ablaze with color. During its descent beyond the horizon, its magnificence was reflected on the waves. The second she turned her head, one of her co-workers stole the remote.

"Hey! I was watchin' that," Kyra whined. The most she had to endure growing up in Chicago was wind and snow - not hurricanes or tornadoes. Such extreme weather proved to be too much for her nerves.

"Girl, relax. It probably won't even hit us." Meeka laughed as though she had no reason to worry.

"I hope you're right. Kyra picked up an old issue of Elle. The last thing she wanted to think about was what could happen if it did. Having escaped the past few Hurricane seasons with only minor damage such as downed power lines and fallen trees, she knew they wouldn't always be so lucky.

"*Oh girl*, would you look at *these*!" A pair of Giuseppe's jumped off the page. Kyra was drawn in by the peep-toe design as well as the dangerously high heel. The rest of the material was covered in tiny rhinestones with larger gold spikes placed throughout. She just had to have them.

"Now those are some bad shoes!" Meeka snatched the magazine away. "How much are they?" she asked.

"More than I can afford," Kyra pouted. Everything about them screamed her name - everything except the price tag. At almost $4,000, they were well out of her price range.

Kyra had never had to check tags before. But, when it was her own money she was spending, things were different. In the past, Kyra wouldn't have batted an eyelash dropping four stacks. When she was with Makai, he actually encouraged her lavish spending habits. It wasn't unheard of for her to spend more than some people made in a year, and she could do it all in one day. Her shopping sprees were legendary.

Fast forward five years and Kyra was lucky if she was able to afford her half of the rent every month. Long gone was the time where all she had to do was snap her fingers to get what she wanted. Now, Kyra worked hard for what she had and there was nothing glamorous about her job as a waitress. She was making chump change compared to the free reign she used to have over limitless credit cards. Her strict budget no longer allowed for her to splurge. She couldn't even afford to go and get her hair and nails done on a whim.

When Kyra came back to Prince Paul, all the perks that came along with the fast life she had grown so accustomed to living came to an end. Once upon a time, Kyra had thousands of dollars at her disposal, but her life as a drug princess quickly turned into a nightmare she couldn't wake up from. It also made it painfully obvious that she couldn't rely on a man to take care of her for the rest of her life. It was time for her to step it up.

As the shock wore off, the harsh reality of Kyra's financial situation began to set in. Jetting off to Chicago cost her everything, including her job at The Butterfly Boutique. Kyra still felt bad about not putting in her two weeks' notice but she hadn't even thought about it until after the fact. By then, it was too late.

When Kyra fell off, she fell hard. She left Chicago with nothing to show for the sacrifices she had made in the name of love. She came home broke, with zero work experience, and no steady income to count on. A decent job was hard to come by and Kyra learned that lesson the hard way. If it weren't for Matthew pulling a few strings, she would probably still be checking the classifieds, praying for an interview.

Eating at Havana's was one thing. Working there was another. Back in the day, Kyra wouldn't have even considered a job in the food industry but, in such a tough economy, she couldn't afford to be picky. Minimum wage was better than nothing. Unlike when she was a teenager, Kyra wasn't working for a living because she wanted to. She had bills to pay.

"Okay ladies, chop, chop! Two of our best servers just called in and the kitchen is already getting backed up. We could really use some coverage out there." Their boss, Christopher, burst in the employee lounge clapping his hands and snapping his fingers as if that would get them to move any faster. Meeka and Kyra just looked at each other.

Break time was officially over.

"Be right out." Kyra stood to fix her uniform. She hated that they were required to wear starchy, long-sleeve shirts, even in the heat. The black pants were a little baggy for her taste, but she still found a way to look somewhat presentable.

"Alright, see you out there," Kyra took a deep breath as she tied her apron tight around her waist. Weekends at Havana's were always super busy, and she was getting ready to walk into the madness that was the dinner rush.

"See ya!" Meeka replied, all up in the mirror. It was clear she was in no hurry to join her. All Kyra could do was shake her head and laugh.

Aside from being her co-worker, Meeka was her girl. She was stop-and-stare pretty, even without makeup. Her skin was the color of dark brown sugar and she wore kinky twists in her hair. Her dark brown eyes were full of life and her sense of humor kept Kyra laughing. When Kyra first started working there, the two of them quickly bonded over their love for designer fashion. That was over three years ago, and they'd been tight ever since.

On her way to the dining area, Kyra cut through the kitchen. Pots and pans dangled from the racks above, and almost everything inside was made of shiny stainless-steel. The amount of space was limited. The heat was immense. It was easy to be overwhelmed by the sights and sounds like the loud fan that seemed to suck all the cool air out of the room, the pop of the fryer, and the sizzle of meat on the grill. Various aromas clashed right along with some of the chef's personalities as they ran back and forth in their white coats and chef hats, giving orders. Their job was to make sure that everything that came out of there looked and smelled amazing. And it always did.

Kyra emerged from the chaos and entered the dining room where the constant clank of silverware mixed with the murmur of conversation. The décor was elegant, with a soaring roof, antique furniture, and crystal chandeliers. The view of the ocean was comparable to the pricey artwork that adorned the walls. A built-in waterfall greeted guests at the entrance.

"Hi, my name is Kyra and I'll be your server this evenin .May I interest you gentlemen in somethin' to drink?" Kyra put on the fakest smile she could manage as she approached a group of distinguished businessmen in suits and ties. No one would've guessed that a little piece of her pride died every time she had to recite that opening line. Kyra had come close to biting the tip of her tongue off on more than one occasion. There were so many times she just wanted to walk out and quit, but she knew she couldn't.

As the night wore on, Kyra found herself juggling several tables with little to no help. She had one woman send her plate back to the kitchen, not once, not twice, but three times. After her steak passed a thorough inspection, she then asked Kyra to bring her a new pair of wine glasses and an extra set of napkins. Her and her husband ran Kyra ragged with their requests, but she made sure to come back and check on them every so often.

After she collected her tips, Kyra took a moment to wipe the sweat from her forehead. She wasn't even halfway through her shift and she was already beat. Her back hurt and her feet were sore, but she wore her smile until her cheeks hurt. She had just finished clearing the table behind a messy party of four, and still had several other hungry guests to attend to.

"Excuse me, waitress!" In the middle of carrying a tub full of dirty dishes to the back, Kyra heard someone call out to her. A little voice inside told her to keep it moving, but her responsibilities wouldn't let her.

"Yes?" Kyra stopped to see what was needed, only to regret it.

Sitting right in front of her was no other than her long-time nemesis, Veronica Pierce.

"Kyra Jones . . . is that you?" Veronica smiled.

"Veronica. . . Hi. . ." Kyra played along when all she really wanted to do was punch her in the face. She didn't know why Veronica was acting so happy to see her. They had never been friends.

"It's been so long! I barely recognized you! How have you been?" Veronica squealed in excitement. Meanwhile, Kyra was trying to come up with any excuse not to talk to her. She continued to scan the room looking for someone - anyone - to come save her, but they were all too busy to notice her suffering.

"Doin' good," Kyra made sure to nod and smile so it sounded more believable, but her appearance offered no support. Kyra had sweat her curls out running back and forth to the kitchen, turning her ponytail into a poof ball. Her uniform was plain except for her apron which had stains on it. Her non-slip shoes were creased and dirty. To sum it up, she looked a hot mess.

For the first time in her life, Kyra felt basic compared to Veronica, who was always so well put together. She secretly envied her Gucci ensemble and the fact she looked like she came straight from the hair salon. Kyra didn't even have to question if the diamonds on her bracelet were real. Her handbag cost more than she made in a month.

"Good for you." Veronica turned to her handsome date.

The way she cut her off, Kyra could tell she didn't really care. Veronica was still the same snooty bitch from high school who thought she was better than her.

"Kyra, I would like for you to meet my boyfriend, Mason Ward." Veronica patted him on the hand to get his attention. Her boyfriend happened to be built like a giant, except he was so quiet it was almost like he wasn't even there. "Mason, honey, this is Kyra. I told you about her. Remember?" she whispered.

Mason simply lifted his glass of cognac in acknowledgement. "Nice to meet you." The way his eyes kept wandering around the room, Kyra got the impression he was bored long before she showed up.

"Good things I hope," Kyra winced at Veronica's little jab. She was trying her best to embarrass her - and it was working. Kyra could only imagine the horrible things Veronica had told him about her; most of which probably weren't even true.

"Why of course!" Veronica did her phony little laugh again; another indication she was lying. "And how is Justin? I haven't heard from him in ages!" she crooned.

"I wouldn't know. We don't really talk." Kyra's eyes drifted to the carpet. Her ex was the one topic she had hoped to avoid. She refused to say her and Justin broke up, because they didn't. They were torn apart, and Kyra still hadn't fully recovered. Underneath every laugh and every smile was this sadness that just wouldn't go away. When it came to Justin, she had scars that would never fade and wounds so deep, she wondered if they would ever heal.

"Oh that's right. I am *so* sorry to hear that." Veronica placed her hand on her heart, as though she felt Kyra's pain.

"Yeah I bet," Kyra held her smile as her anger boiled to the surface. Eighteen-year-old Kyra would've jumped across the table right then - and wouldn't have felt bad about it. But the more mature Kyra swallowed her insults, no matter how clever.

"Well it was nice talking to you." The tray on her shoulder provided the perfect exit when she started to wobble under its weight.

"Oh, and Kyra, before you go would you mind fetching me a refill? Thanks." Veronica added her glass to the pile before shooing her away like a pest.

No she didn't! As soon as Kyra turned around her eyelids flickered. She marched straight to the back, cursing under her breath.

"*Dang!* Who pissed you off?" Meeka stopped on her way to the floor.

"That girl over there. . ." Kyra glared in Veronica's direction.

Meeka sucked her teeth. "She's been coming in a lot lately. . . Acts like she owns the place. . . What'd she do? You need me to say something? 'Cause I will. . ." Meeka made it clear from the start of their friendship that if Kyra ever had a problem she was the first person to call. A hot head just like her, Meeka was two seconds away from taking off her earrings and busting out the Vaseline. All Kyra had to do was say the word.

"No, don't say anythin'. I don't want you to get in trouble," Kyra objected. Her petty beef wasn't worth either one of them losing their job. Unlike Veronica, neither of them had a fluffy trust fund to fall back on.

"You should spit in her food," Meeka's suggestion came with an evil grin.

"No!" Kyra laughed out loud. The visual that formed in her mind was almost worth it.

"What? That's what I would do," Meeka shrugged and walked off.

Kyra seriously thought about it, too. She even thought about getting Veronica the refill she asked for and pouring it on her, but as much as Kyra would have loved to repay Veronica for the horrible way she treated her over the years, she had more important things to tend to. Her revenge would have to wait.

After checking off everything on the list of closing duties at the end of the night, Kyra was exhausted. Eight hours on her feet took its toll on her body, and by the end of her shift it seemed like everything ached. Not to mention, her last customers of the night left her nothing but a headache. She had been ready to go hours ago.

A steady downpour began just moments after Kyra left the restaurant, and its force further wore on her nerves. The rain was falling so hard and with such speed it made it hard to see, but she was determined to reach her destination. A short boat ride to Prince Paul was the only thing standing between Kyra and the one thing she wanted most – her bed. However, due to the storm, ferry service had been cut short and, of course, the boat Kyra needed was delayed. She should have been home in a matter of minutes and yet happiness seemed so far away, Kyra wondered if she would ever know what it was like to be truly happy again.

It wasn't unusual for her to go home feeling like she hated her job, but tonight, she was sure of it. Sitting alone in her car gave Kyra all the time she needed to reflect on her day, and even though it had been hours since she crossed paths with Veronica, she was still heated. Last she knew, Veronica got shipped off to some boarding school in Europe right along with her good-for-nothing brother Richard, and as far as she was concerned, she could've stayed there. Kyra hadn't seen Veronica since their days at the academy. If she never saw Veronica again it would still be too soon.

And she just had to bring up Justin. Kyra couldn't believe she had the nerve. Veronica knew that her and Justin weren't together anymore. She was part of the reason why. Not to mention, Veronica had been throwing shade ever since Kyra moved to Prince Paul. Kyra was sure that when Veronica heard about the circumstances surrounding their breakup, it was just something else for her to gossip about. The only reason Veronica was asking her all those questions was so she could be all up in her business.

Unfortunately for Kyra, all it took was even the slightest mention of Justin to conjure up memories she had been long trying to suppress. She still had her share of regrets stemming from that fateful summer in The Chi, as well as the consequences that seemed to linger long after. As hard as she tried to forget it ever happened, she would never be able to forget what it was like holding him in her arms while praying for God to spare his life as he lay bleeding in the middle of the street.

Kyra would never forget the last time she saw Justin. No matter how hard she tried to block it out, that night kept playing over and over again in her mind. All she had to do was close her eyes and it was like she was there. Even after all these years, it was still so vivid, so real.

I still remember wakin' up in the hospital. I'm not sure how long I was out, but the second I opened my eyes, I thought to check on Justin. I expected to see him lyin' next to me, except he wasn't there. There was no trace of him. It was as if he had disappeared.

Assumin' the worst, I rushed out into the hallway where I was stopped by a nurse. She kept tellin' me to quiet down, but she pissed me off when she refused to take me to him. I begged and pleaded with her for information, but that lady was less than sympathetic. Only family was allowed to discuss that kind of stuff and she had no problem pointin' out that I was only his "girlfriend."

That was right around the time my mom decided to show up, Matthew in tow. Both of them looked burnt out, like they hadn't slept in days. Even Matthew looked worried. It wasn't until then that I began to realize my decision to go to Chicago had had an effect on everybody - not just me.

The moment I laid eyes on my mom, I was overcome by a mixture of fear and relief. I begged the police not to call her, but there was no gettin' out of it. Given the fact that Justin and I were both minors at the time, they were required to notify our parents.

I dreaded my mom's reaction from the time I found out she was comin' to get me. Probably even more than the possibility of goin' to jail. But at the same time, I was glad to have her there. I thought she was goin' to be so mad at me so I was pretty shocked when she didn't yell at me or cuss me out. She just hugged me and cried.

And I cried right along with her until I spotted Mr. Hartwell headed toward us, lookin' like he was ready to mow me or anybody else over in his path. The fear in my heart stopped my tears the moment the hallway turned into a battlefield. On one side was my family, ready to protect and support me. On the other was Justin's family, ready to tear me down.

"Now you listen to me because I am going to only say this once!" Mr. Harwell roared, his eyes wild. "Whatever it is you thought you and my son had going on is over as of today! You are not to come anywhere near him or anyone in this family! You set so much as a foot on my property and I will have you arrested for trespassing! Do I make myself clear?" The boom in his voice had my stomach doin' back flips. I was so upset I couldn't even get a sentence out. An apology wasn't nearly enough.

Mrs. Hartwell even went on to call me nothin' but a "trouble maker" and said Justin was a fool to ever fall for a "ghetto girl" like me. I looked to Quentin, hopin' he might vouch for me, and got nothin' more than an angry look. The way he clenched his jaw let me know he didn't have anything nice to contribute.

Once our parents started hurlin' insults back and forth, security stepped in and told us we had to leave, but I refused to go quietly. They literally had to drag me out, kickin' and screamin.' So what if I looked crazy? I didn't care. I cried the whole way home, and for what seemed *like days afterward.*

I was lucky to be alive, even if I didn't feel like it at the time. I had survived Makai's abuse, but horrible nightmares plagued my sleep for months. The stress ate at me so bad I lost an unhealthy amount of weight. I even lost some hair. When I lost Justin, I almost lost my mind, too.

Ugh! I still don't understand how I wasted so much time on a guy like Makai. He never really cared about me. When he showed up on out of nowhere, beggin' me to take him back, I should've known somethin' was up. After he dogged me out the way he did, I should've been up on game.

But I was just so mad at Justin, and so hurt. I let my anger get the best of me. When he got back with Veronica, Makai's offer ended up being an easy way out. That's all it was. It was convenient. So I took it. Trustin' Makai was easily the biggest mistake I ever made.

Eager to get home and escape the bad weather, Kyra made sure she was one of the first to board the last ferry of the night but, as soon as they pulled away from the dock, the angry sea tossed the boat about like a toy. Gripping the steering wheel tight, she said a silent prayer asking God to get her home safely. Her heart was beating so fast and so hard it almost felt as if all the blood in her body had rushed to it at once.

I wouldn't say I'm happy that Makai is dead but, after the shit he put me through, it's not like I cry about it. Honestly, it feels good to know he can't hurt me anymore. I can go to sleep at night and not have to worry where he is or what he is doin'. He can't come after me this time.

I still don't know what is more shockin': the fact that Makai is really gone or that he took his own life. I can still see the look in his eyes as he raised the barrel to his temple. If he was scared to pull the trigger, he didn't look it. One minute he was there, and the next, he was gone.

Not only did Makai lose his younger brother to the streets, he was losin' his war with Reggie, and a truce was out of the question. Knowin' Makai, his ego would've never allowed it. There was no way he was ever going to surrender and his pride would never accept defeat. Rather than spend the rest of his life in prison, I guess he saw death as his only escape.

Kai was only 18 when he committed suicide. He lasted a lot longer than most, though. Prior to his death, he was known as one of Chi-town's most notorious gangsters, as cold and ruthless as they come. And while he certainly earned that reputation, everybody knows once the game turns on you there's nothin' you can do. No one is untouchable.

I watched Makai fall apart, right along with the empire he worked so hard to build. Every police officer in the city knew him by name and the Feds had gotten wind of his drug operation. It was only a matter of time before he got caught. If he was goin' down, then he was goin' to take everybody else down with him. He almost succeeded, too.

Kyra was jolted from her dreamlike state by the attendant knocking on her window. They would be pulling into port in a matter of minutes, however she had been so consumed by her thoughts she was the last to notice.

As Kyra slowed to a stop in front of Colony Park, her apartment complex, her mind went into overdrive thinking about everything Justin. It seemed like the more she tried not to think about him the more she thought about him. She couldn't help but wonder what he was doing at that very moment: Where was he? Was he happy? Was there any chance he missed her as much as she missed him? Kyra thought about Justin all the time - which was way more than she should have because she already had a man.

Kyra started dating Cincere over a year ago. Problem was she was still unsure of her feelings for him. Yes, Kyra cared deeply about him. He had been there for her when nobody else was. When she talked, he listened. He accepted Kyra and her past: the good and the bad. In their time together, his love for her had proved unconditional. And still, Kyra couldn't find it in her heart to love him the way she knew he deserved to be loved.

By all accounts, Cincere was a good, respectable guy. He had a legit job working construction and Kyra appreciated the fact she no longer had to worry about the police knocking down their door at four in the morning or being shot at. He was an honest man, who never made her question where he was at night. But did she love him like she loved Justin? Not even close.

Kyra let him know she could care less about a title, but Cincere seemed dead-set on cuffing her. She told him she wasn't ready for anything serious when they first met, and somehow, she still ended up in a relationship. After they moved in together, Kyra felt like she was on a speeding train that was destined to crash, with no way of getting off.

Playing house was fun at first, but it didn't take long for her to see that domestic bliss wasn't all it was cracked up to be. Once Cincere was sure he had her, he didn't put in much effort to keep her. When they weren't having sex, Kyra wondered where they were going and how much longer they would last.

However, the second she flung open the door to her domain, Kyra was worry-free. At that moment, nothing else mattered. She made it. She was home.

"Oh, shit! Did you see that?" Cincere was entranced by the flat screen mounted on the wall. An avid fan of UFC, it was almost eleven o'clock at night, and he was shouting at the TV.

"Can you keep it down? I have a headache."

Kyra was further annoyed when she found a pile of dirty dishes waiting for her in the sink.

"Hey, babe, what are we having for dinner?" Living the last moments of the match, Cincere's eyes were still glued to the screen. Another loud outburst came soon after.

"Hell yeah, that's what the fuck I'm talking about!" Cincere jumped to his feet and started clapping.

Kyra rolled her eyes.

"Work was great. Thanks for askin'."

She set her bags down on the counter and drew a deep breath. Coming home and cooking for him was the last thing she felt like doing, but she was in no mood to argue.

"Humph, I don't know what kind of gourmet meal he thinks he's getting' at this time of night. . ." Kyra transferred the leftovers she had snagged from the restaurant from a plastic container to a plate. Standing there with her arms folded, waiting for the microwave to ding, she couldn't help but think about how nice it would be if Cincere made dinner for once, but she knew better than to hold her breath. The second Kyra set his food in front of him Cincere started attacking it like he hadn't eaten all day. He didn't even utter so much as a "Thank you."

After the day she had, Kyra couldn't wait to strip down and barricade herself in the bathroom. She closed her eyes and let her muscles relax as the warm water flowed over her body. As she washed off all the dirt and grease from the day, she let go of all the anger and frustration that came along with it. When she was finished, she rung out her hair, but when Kyra reached for her towel her hand was met by the towel rack.

"What in the . . . ? I could've sworn I put it right there. . ." she felt around blindly.

"Cincere, can you bring me a towel?" Kyra snatched back the shower curtain to confirm her towel was indeed missing. When she didn't get an answer, she yelled louder.

"Cincere?" When he still didn't answer her, Kyra took it upon herself to go looking for him.

"Do I have to do everythin' around here," Kyra grumbled as she stepped out of the shower. The second the air hit her skin, her whole body was covered in goosebumps.

"Cincere, I know you hear me callin' you!" Kyra stomped from room to room, tracking wet footprints through each. The first place she checked was the living room, then the kitchen, but there was no sign of Cincere. All the lights were off.

"There you are." Kyra's search finally came to an end in the bedroom, where she found Cincere sitting shirtless on the corner of the bed. He had her towel in his hand and a mischievous smirk that only meant one thing.

"Looking for something?" The sound of his voice was almost as seductive as the look in his eyes. The way he licked his lips dared her to make the first move.

"Boy, I know you heard me callin' you," Kyra put her hand on her hip and cracked a sassy smile. The flicker of candlelight made her skin glisten.

"Can I have my towel back now? I'm cold." Kyra shivered, but for a different reason. Even though Cincere was a few inches shorter than Justin, his looks were far above average. His slanted eyes were intriguing hints of his African-American-Korean heritage and his skin was the color of a Hershey's Kiss. His mustache was thin and there was no trace of a beard on his baby face. Many of his features were reminiscent of a young Tyson Beckford, and his body was just as nice.

"You just sit back and relax. . . Let me do it." Cincere hid the towel behind his back every time she tried to take it from him. Starting at her feet and working his way up her legs, he ran the soft cloth over her calves and along the back of her thighs, careful not to leave a drop of water behind. The sensations he created with a single kiss in between her shoulder blades had Kyra weak already. She even let a moan slip.

Cincere took his time chasing the tiny droplets as they maneuvered around her many curves, making sure to lick up any water he might have missed. He planted delicate kisses up her spine while admiring every inch of her nakedness.

"Turn over." His trail of kisses ended just below her ear. The tone he used had Kyra gripping the sheets and he wasn't even inside her yet. Just when Kyra thought Cincere was done teasing her, he started the process over, except this time, his big, strong hands roamed her body freely, making sure to massage in every last bit of lotion.

"*Mm*, you missed a spot," Kyra bit her lip as he ran his hand between her thighs. He touched her everywhere except the one place she was longing to be touched.

"That's okay. I'm only going to make it wet again anyway." Cincere looked at her like he meant every word.

"Promises, promises. . . " Kyra flashed a naughty smirk. She initiated the first kiss, but Cincere wouldn't let her stop there. He found something about her kisses to be addictive. No matter how many she gave him, he couldn't get enough.

Like animals in heat, rolling around on the bed, feeding off each other's desires, Kyra gasped for air when he found her entrance. His first stroke was slow and deep. It seemed like every movement was deliberate and calculated, as each position flowed seamlessly into the next. Cincere knew exactly how to handle her. He knew exactly what to say.

Cincere continued to grind deep inside her, causing Kyra to moan loud enough for their neighbors to hear. He whispered for her to be quiet, but Kyra was feeling too good to care. Watching him glide in and out of her only heightened her urge to scream.

Encouraged by the sounds she was making, Cincere dove to the depths of her wetness, soaking the sheets. He helped himself to a handful of curls, and began thrusting so fast, he seemed unstoppable. Cincere pushed himself to the limit, and Kyra begged him not to slow down.

Stillness fell over the room as the young lovers lay fitted together like puzzle pieces in the dark afterward. Spent from their love making, Cincere fell asleep almost instantly, but the steady sound of rain hitting the roof did little to soothe Kyra. As the storm raged on outside, she clung to the comfort that came with being in her boyfriend's arms even though part of her still wished it was Justin in his place. Every night she closed her eyes, Kyra hoped to see him in her dreams.

CHAPTER 2

"Good morning," Cincere gurgled, still half asleep. It was well past noon when he rolled out of bed and staggered into the living room, scratching his chest.

"Hey, it's about time you got up! The day's half over!" Kyra danced her way over to him with a big smile on her face. Fresh air filled the room along with a little 90's R&B. She had been busy cleaning all morning.

"Wow babe, the apartment looks great," Cincere complimented her hard work. "I hope this means you're not still mad at me." His hands rested on her hips.

"You know I could never stay mad at you." Kyra followed up with a kiss to convince him.

"Are you hungry? I can always fix you somethin' if you want." Kyra rarely offered to cook, but after the way he put it down, he didn't even have to ask.

"Sure. Thanks, babe," Cincere sought out his favorite spot on the couch and kicked back.

Meanwhile, Kyra got busy rummaging through all the cabinets, only to discover that minus a couple spices and a stale pack of ramen noodles, they were bare. She opened the fridge only to find that too, was empty.

"Damn. Looks I'll have to run to the store. I'll be right back." Kyra grabbed her keys and blew Cincere a kiss on her way out.

For the first time in a long time, Kyra stepped out into the muggy Caribbean day without thinking twice about her outfit. She was wearing one of Cincere's old Bob Marley T-shirts, a pair of faded, cut-off jeans, and a bandana to hide her messy bun. Normally, there was no way she would set foot out the house dressed like that, but Kyra figured she was just making a quick trip to the grocery store. It wasn't that big of a deal. Besides, it wasn't like she had anyone to impress.

Kyra turned the key in the ignition and the old Jeep Cherokee rumbled to life. It had been passed down to her after she graduated and, even though it was used, it was still pretty reliable. Other than the fact that the air conditioning stopped working last summer and neither she nor Cincere had the money to fix it, she hadn't had to take it to a mechanic for any other reason. And while it might not have been as nice as the cars she would have liked to own, it got her from point A to point B, which was all that mattered.

En route to the nearest convenience store, Kyra decided to take a detour through her old neighborhood. She drove for miles until she spotted the house she was looking for. The bright blue paint made it almost impossible to miss, and the white wraparound porch was just as impressive as it was the first time she saw it. Kyra couldn't help but reminisce every time she rode by.

So much about my life has changed since we moved here, it's like my brain is still tryin' to process it. After mom re-married, I guess I was so focused on the fact that Matthew was gonna be my step-dad, that I completely overlooked the fact we would be livin' under the same roof, let alone who's roof that would be. It didn't take long after they said "I do" for them to put a For Sale sign in our yard. Before I knew it, we were movin' - again.

Needless to say, my last year at home was a real struggle. Livin' under my mother's constant surveillance 24/7 caused a lot of arguments. I was the only 18-year-old I knew who wasn't allowed to go anywhere or do anythin' by myself. There were some days it seemed like I couldn't even breathe without her questionin' her or accusin' me of lyin' about somethin.' It's been years, and I still feel like I'm workin' to regain her trust.

Me and Tasha are still connected on Facebook, but after the foul ass shit she did, that's the extent of our friendship. We hardly ever talk on there, and Angel won't talk to me at all. She made it obvious she sided with Quentin and his family. While I understand her position, I still wish she would've at least cared to get my side of the story before she made her decision.

The only person I have seen since I got back is Michael, who I manage to avoid. And then there's Mercedes. Even after losin' her daughter, she still hasn't changed her ways. I really wasn't even surprised to learn she had been showin' her goods on Worldstar. I saw the videos to prove it.

I tried lookin' Justin up online, but out of the thousands of Justins that came up in my search, none of them were my Justin. I swear I've checked every social site out there, but it's useless. I can't find him anywhere, and I'm beginnin' to think maybe that's because he doesn't want to be found.

Kyra pulled off in deep thought. She knew it was important that she cherish the good times she shared with Justin, because in the end, that's all she had left. Sadly, when it came to every man she ever loved all Kyra had left were memories.

As I've gotten older, I've come to realize that losin' my father isn't somethin' I'll ever get over. It's somethin' I had to learn to live with. Gettin' his initials tattooed on my wrist is my way of keepin' him close. It also serves as a reminder that no matter how hard life gets, my guardian angel will never abandon me. My father sacrificed his life for me, and for *that I am forever grateful.*

People say my father is in a better place, but that doesn't mean I still don't yearn to see justice served. I have every right to be angry, I haven't figured out where to direct it. I need someone to blame, but who? My mom? My dad? The system? Me? The betrayal by the authorities cut deep considerin' my father was gunned down in broad daylight and nothin' was done about it.

I just hope that someday, I'll be able to put a face on the man who took my father's life and changed mine forever. I wanna be able to look him in the eye and tell him exactly what I think of him. I want to know he finally got what he deserved. And most importantly, I want someone else to suffer, just as much as I have. I need to know they feel an ounce of the pain I feel, day in and day out.

Kyra was still trying to get a grip on her emotions when she stepped out of the car. She marched up to the convenience store doors and tugged on the handles, only to find them locked. She hadn't noticed the "Gone to Lunch" sign hanging in the window until she got up close. The hands on the clock said they weren't due back for another thirty minutes.

"Ugh! You cannot be serious right now!" Kyra pressed her face against the glass. It was too dark to see inside.

"Hello! Is anybody in there?" She tried pulling on the doors again and was met by resistance.

"Damn it!" Kyra got back in the Jeep and slammed the door behind her. Her next best option was the farmer's market all the way on the other side of Prince Paul.

Overcast blanketed the island, stripping it of its vibrant colors and replacing them with dull shades of gray. The sun played hide-and-seek amongst the clouds while Kyra moseyed from stall to stall chatting with each of the different vendors, filling her basket to with fresh ingredients. Once it got too heavy to carry, Kyra decided to lug her purchases back to the car, when she spotted a familiar face in the crowd that left her breathless.

Were her eyes deceiving her? Could it be true? Standing just a few feet away from her was the one and only Justin Hartwell, and needless to say he was looking *too* good.

Kyra took in every little detail like she was seeing Justin again for the first time, from his beautiful brown eyes to his breathtaking smile. She was happy to see him looking so strong and healthy. The way he kept laughing and smiling let her know he was happy, too. At least she hoped he was.

It was funny because Justin looked exactly the same as he did when Kyra last saw him only, better. He was slightly taller than she remembered, and the outlines of his muscles were visible beneath his shirt. Always so clean shaven, Kyra was surprised to see he had grown a scruffy beard that covered most of his face.

Justin must've felt her staring because the carefree expression on his face went blank. The moment they locked eyes was so intense, Kyra thought she was about to faint. In a crowd full of people, they had still managed to find each other. Once they made eye contact, neither let go.

Their attraction to each other was still so magnetic Justin couldn't resist making his way over. But instead of running toward him with arms wide open, Kyra nearly dropped everything trying to get away. One look down at what she was wearing and she panicked. After not seeing him for so long she couldn't afford to make a bad impression. There was no way she was going to let him see her looking hit.

"Kyra!" Justin waved to her, but Kyra sped off as though she were being chased. She didn't know where she was going nor did she care, all she knew for sure was she had to get out of there. Her eyes didn't leave the rearview until she was sure her past couldn't catch up to her.

Overcome with emotion, Kyra had to pull over on the side of the road. Seeing Justin in person brought up a lot of emotions she wasn't ready to deal with. The two of them fell out so long ago it didn't make sense to cry about it, but it was like she didn't have a choice. She couldn't stop the tears from coming. Every time she wiped them more came.

Running into Justin only reminded Kyra of how much she missed him. It didn't matter how much time passed, being apart wasn't getting any easier for her. Each day without him seemed longer than the last. Days turned into weeks. Weeks turned into months. Months turned into years, but her love for Justin never waned.

Kyra grunted in frustration. As soon as she had the chance to tell him how she felt, she blew it. She let him slip away.

Kyra even tried to convince herself that the man she saw wasn't Justin just to make herself feel better. But deep down, she knew that was a lie.

"Hey, girl, what's up? Is everything okay?" The look on Meeka's face was one of confusion and concern. The second she opened the door Kyra blew past her and made herself at home on the couch.

"No. Everything is not okay!" Kyra's bloodshot eyes were a dead giveaway that she had been crying. She had held her composure just long enough to make it there.

"Aw, what's wrong? Why are you crying?" Meeka sounded like she was on the verge herself.

"I just ran into Justin." One look in Kyra's eyes revealed her heartbreak.

"Francesca! Stop it!" Meeka scolded Francesca, her beloved Chihuahua, for interrupting as she scooped her up off the floor. Once she made herself comfortable on her owner's lap, Francesca seemed to calm down.

"Hold up. Wait a minute . . . *Rewind*! Justin? As in your long lost *ex-boyfriend* Justin?" Meeka's jaw dropped.

"Yes!" Kyra shot up out of her seat. Both her voice and her hands were shaking uncontrollably.

"Where did you see him?"

"At the marketplace . . . Not even an hour ago," she rambled.

"And you're sure it was him?" Meeka squinted.

"Yes, I'm sure!"

"Did he say anything?"

"He called my name!" Kyra squealed.

"Well, did you talk to him? What did he say?" Meeka pet her dog while she talked.

"No! As soon as I saw him I left," Kyra confessed.

"What do you mean you left? Why didn't you talk to him?" Meeka chuckled.

"It's not like I was expectin' to see him. Great! Now, he probably thinks I'm crazy." Kyra worried.

"Oh, I'm sure it wasn't that bad," Meeka laughed off her dramatics.

"Ugh! I am just so mad at myself for not sayin' anythin'! I can't tell you how many times I planned what I would do if I ever saw him again. Today I finally had my chance, and I ruined it!" Kyra put her face in her hands.

"So if you didn't even talk to him then how do you know for sure it was him? For all you know, you could be getting yourself all worked up over nothing," Meeka pointed out.

"I can't explain how I know. I just know."

Even after a quick touch-up on her hair and makeup, Kyra was reluctant to head back home. Knowing Cincere had been waiting close to an hour, she was prepared for an argument as soon as she walked in, but when he met her at the door, he took the heavy load off her hands.

"Hey it's about time you got back. I'm starving," he said.

"Sorry I took so long. The store was closed so I had to drive all the way to the farmer's market," her explanation came with a heavy sigh. She didn't even feel like cooking anymore.

"I'm just glad you're home. I was starting to worry about you." Cincere wrapped his arms around her, but Kyra broke free from him.

"Babe, what's wrong? Are you okay?" Cincere looked confused as to how she went from being loving and affectionate to cold and distant in the short time she was gone.

"I said I'm fine." Kyra concentrated on putting the groceries away instead of making eye-contact. She didn't want him to pick up on the fact that she had been crying and start asking questions.

That same night, just before bed, Kyra dug out an old picture of her and Justin in Jamaica. She knew she probably shouldn't still have pictures of him since she was with Cincere, but she just couldn't bring herself to throw them away. Unlike Makai, Justin was someone she actually wanted to remember.

When they were together, Justin wasn't just her lover, he was her best friend. No matter who else came along, she would always have love for him. The longer she studied his face, the more she wished she could relive their first night together. Kyra closed her eyes and let her imagination run wild as she molded her body to her biggest, fluffiest pillow.

"What you got there?"

Kyra nearly jumped out her skin at the sound of Cincere's voice. Lost in her trance, she hadn't noticed him come in.

"Oh nothin'. . . . Just looking at some old pictures . . ." As soon as she felt tears coming, Kyra put her memories of Justin back in the shoebox, and slid it back under the bed.

"You still miss him don't you?" Cincere cradled her face in his hands, using his thumbs to dry her cheeks. It hurt his heart to see her so unhappy.

"Every day," Kyra fought to keep her composure. A smile concealed her pain, but gazing in his eyes did nothing to ebb her growing sense of guilt. She knew his question was in reference to her father, just like she knew she could never tell him the truth.

"Don't worry. You'll always have me." Cincere lent her his shoulder to cry on and gave her his heart to keep. But when he told her he loved her, Kyra couldn't even give him that.

CHAPTER 3

Kyra found peace in her sleep. In the morning, Cincere left early to go jogging so she was thoroughly enjoying having their king size bed all to herself. It seemed like she had just gotten comfortable when she was startled by a knock at the door.

"Ugh, it is too early for this shit!" Kyra pulled the covers over her head. She even put a pillow over her ears, hoping that if she ignored them they would go away, but whoever it was, they sure were persistent.

"Just a minute." Kyra hated to part with her mattress. She rolled over, checked her phone, and let out another groan. It was just after 9 A.M. She wasn't expecting company and Cincere wouldn't be home from his workout for at least another hour. Any other time, she would have gone with him, but yesterday's events left her feeling so physically and emotionally drained she had decided to stay behind and catch up on some much needed rest. *So much for that*, she thought.

"I said I'm comin'! Hold on!" Kyra tied her robe closed, confused about who was crazy enough to wake her up so early on her day off. By the time she was done with them, they would know better than to ever bother her again.

"What the hell do you want?" Kyra flung the door open.

Earth stood still and time stopped.

"Justin? . . . What are you doin' here?" Kyra was stuck. There was her ex-boyfriend, dressed casually in a pair of expensive designer jeans and T-shirt, looking sexy as ever. His hairline was extra crispy, and his scruff had been neatly shaped into a goatee. Everything about him from his car to his clothes was clean.

"Sorry for just showing up like this. I wasn't quite sure how to get in touch with you." Justin rushed to get the words out. One look in her eyes and he almost forgot what he going to say.

"How did you find me?" Kyra stepped forward.

"You - uh - dropped this in your hurry yesterday. I figured you might need it." Justin removed a small plastic card from his pocket, which upon closer inspection, turned out to be Kyra's driver's license.

"Oh wow! Thank you! I'm glad it was you who found it." She diverted her eyes in embarrassment. Kyra had been so caught up in him, she wasn't even aware it was missing.

"You're welcome," Justin cleared his throat, unsure what to say next.

As Kyra and Justin stood there staring at each other in disbelief, an awkward silence fell over them. The minutes passed excruciatingly slow.

"You want to come inside?" Kyra stepped aside to welcome him in.

"I would, but I'm already running late for my meeting." Justin glanced at his Rolex with regret. "Maybe we can catch up some other time? You know, have dinner or something." His suggestion was hopeful.

"Okay. Yeah. Sure," Kyra fumbled over her answer. She was willing to meet him on the moon if he asked her to.

"Okay. Cool. Here's my number. Give me a call and we'll set something up." Justin held his card up between her fingers.

"You take care, Kyra." There was no denying their hug lasted a few seconds longer than it should of. The temptation to kiss was present and growing by the second, and if Justin didn't leave soon, Kyra wasn't sure how much longer she could fight it.

"You, too," Kyra put on a smile, but watching him walk back to his car, left her fighting tears. And for some reason when it came to Justin, that was a battle she never seemed to win.

As much as Kyra enjoyed spending time with him, seeing him go was always bittersweet. She was just so happy to finally have him back she couldn't fathom what it would be like to lose him again. It seemed almost unfair to have to say goodbye so soon considering every time she saw Justin, she had to question whether it would be the last.

Once back inside, Kyra screamed like she won the lottery. Except what she gained was more valuable than money. When Justin gave her his business card, Kyra took it as him giving her much more than just a piece of paper. He was giving her a second chance.

Lost in a daze, Kyra dove onto her mattress face-first. Her excitement erupted in a girly shriek as she kicked her feet up in the air. This was just too good to keep secret. She had to tell someone.

Kyra pulled up outside Meeka's house moments later. And while the mat at the front door welcomed company, the voice on the other end didn't sound as inviting.

"Who is it?" Meeka spied through the peephole.

"It's me! Open up!" Kyra pounded harder.

"Kyra, you have got to stop popping up like this. Do you have any idea what time it is?" Meeka cracked the door just wide enough to let her in.

"Sorry! I know. I should've called first, but you will never guess what just happened!" Kyra flopped on the couch.

"What is it? Because you better have a damn good reason for waking me up at the crack of dawn," Meeka sounded grouchy. In her world, nothing was that exciting that early in the morning.

"Justin came by my house this morning!" Kyra blurted out what she thought was good news, but Meeka sounded more skeptical than anything.

"Is he crazy? What if Cincere had been there?"

"I know! Luckily he wasn't," Kyra went quiet. She didn't even want to imagine how things would have played out had Cincere been the one to answer the door.

"Well, what did he want?" Meeka sat down, ready to listen.

"He brought me my I.D," Kyra smiled at the memory.

"*Aw.* Isn't that sweet?" Meeka teased.

"I don't know how I lost it. I must've dropped it leavin' the market yesterday." Kyra shook her head in embarrassment.

"Did he say anything about what happened?" Meeka yawned.

"No. Thank God." Kyra sighed in relief. Meeka on the other hand, couldn't stop laughing.

"Meeka *stop!* It's not funny!" Kyra tried her best to hold in her laugh, but even she got a good chuckle out of it.

"Okay! Okay! But that's not all." Kyra tapped Meeka to be quiet. "Before he left, he asked me out to dinner!" Kyra couldn't hide her smile if she tried. No one could make her swoon like Justin. Not even some of the finest celebrities.

"Say what!" Meeka's pitch spiked with surprise. She was up now.

"I know right!" Kyra bounced up and down in her seat.

"So are you going to go or what?" Meeka posed the most important question of their conversation and suddenly, the topic turned serious.

"Oh. Well, yeah. Of course I'm gonna go," Kyra replied as though Meeka was crazy for asking. There was no way she was going to turn Justin down.

"And might I ask what *Cincere* thinks about all of this?" Meeka raised an eyebrow with her next question. Kyra hadn't even thought about her boyfriend, nor did she care to be reminded.

"He doesn't know yet." Kyra turned away from Meeka's judgment.

"Well, aren't you going to tell him?" Meeka asked.

"No. I don't know. Do you think I should?" Kyra weighed her options. If she told Cincere about Justin stopping by that would just create drama – and drama was the last thing she needed.

"Kyra," Meeka gasped at her decision.

"What? Justin and I are just friends. It's not like anythin' is goin' to happen," Kyra summed it up as though it were really that simple. When in reality, the sexual tension between her and Justin was so thick at times it made it hard to breathe.

"Cincere is your boyfriend," Meeka filled in for Kyra's conscience.

"So!" The look on Kyra's face made it clear she could care less.

"Kyra, you need to tell him. He deserves to know." Meeka argued.

"Um, excuse me, I thought you were *my* friend. Since when are you on his side?" Kyra's irritation gave way to hopelessness. "And besides, even if I do say somethin' you and I both know he'll never let me go," she sighed.

"I say ask him. See what he says. You never know. He might surprise you," Meeka advised.

"Yeah. . . Maybe. . ." Kyra sounded doubtful to say the least. While she had vowed not to keep secrets from Cincere, she knew him well enough to know that he would never agree. Kyra was sure once she told Cincere her plans, their conversation would end in an argument. It was best for her not to say anything until she absolutely had to and only *if* she had to.

"Look, I don't know what you're about to do, but I'm about to go back to sleep. This is way too much for my brain to process this early in the morning," Meeka got up and stretched.

"What do you think I should do?" Kyra stopped in the doorway.

"I don't know. Whatever you decide, that's on you. If you feel like going to dinner with Justin is the right thing to do then do it. All I'm saying is just remember every action has a reaction . . . even love has its consequences."

Kyra heard Meeka's warning loud and clear. She simply chose not to listen. Kyra went against everything Meeks told her the moment she decided to follow her heart.

CHAPTER 4

To call or not to call; that was the question Kyra struggled with over the course of the next three days. The answer seemed so cut and dry, but then there were times where she felt like Meeka was right. Cincere hadn't done anything wrong. He didn't deserve to be mistreated.

Kyra had been loyal thus far, but this was something she couldn't ignore. If she didn't at least call, she knew she would never forgive herself. Besides, it wasn't like she couldn't call Justin. She didn't really have a choice. After all he had done for her, she owed him that much. Dinner was the least she could do.

Kyra was so conflicted over Justin's proposal it made it hard for her to concentrate on even the simplest tasks at work. She was late for her shift the day after he came to visit. The day after that she kept mixing up people's orders, and the day after that she dropped a stack of dishes. All her co-workers were asking questions and her boss even threatened to fire her if she didn't shape up. Kyra was having the worst week ever but all she could think about was how bad she wanted to see Justin again.

Justin's business card was hidden in her panty drawer, where she knew Cincere would never find it. Kyra snuck off to peek at it every chance she got. She kept telling herself that a quick phone call was harmless, but that didn't stop her from getting nervous. It was a lot of pressure knowing she held all the power about moving forward. One phone call had the power to change everything which was why it was so scary. Their future was in her hands.

Kyra repeated Justin's number until she knew it by heart. Late one night after Cincere fell asleep in front of the TV she finally took the opportunity to use it. She locked the door to their bedroom as a precaution. He could wake up at any minute which meant she had to make it quick.

Her breathing was suspended as she held the phone to her ear. The ringing seemed to go on forever but Kyra wasn't giving up until she got an answer. As she waited for Justin to pick up, she couldn't help but wonder if she would finally get the get the answers she had been looking for? And even if she did, was she ready to hear them? Could she handle the truth?

Come Friday night, Kyra couldn't wait to pluck her new BeBe mini-dress off the hanger. A $159.00 dollar price tag hung next to the jeweled trim and she had been waiting anxiously to pop it. It had been sitting in her closet so long she almost forgot she had it.

The dress was the epitome of sexy and perfect for the occasion. The long sleeves had slits in them that ran all the way down her arms and the material fit her so well it was as though it had been made exclusively for her. Its length - or lack thereof - accentuated her long legs while the open back left most of her back exposed.

"Hey, babe I'll be back later." The first time Kyra mentioned she was leaving, she was already on the way out.

"*Mm, Mm, Mm!* Damn girl, where you going dressed like that?" Cincere did a double take when she walked past. After spending hours in the bathroom getting ready for her dinner date, Kyra was smelling good and looking better. She had painted her nails pale pink and her usually curly hair was bone straight. Other than foundation and mascara, she didn't have on a lot of make-up. She didn't need to add any flashy jewelry, just a pair of rhinestone studs. Her black clutch matched perfectly, and a pair of strappy sandals from BCBG spruced up her look.

"Out to dinner with a friend," Kyra kept her answers short. She had agreed to meet Justin at the Coco Bistro in ten minutes and it was going to take her at least twenty to get there.

"And who is this 'friend?'"

Cincere got up to confront her.

"Just an old friend from high school." Kyra stopped to admire her ensemble in the full-length mirror.

"Who?" Cincere kept the questions coming. A brief pause in conversation only added to their tension.

"Justin." Kyra stopped to look at him. The second she said his name, Cincere's facial expression changed.

"Whoa! Hold up! Did I miss something? I thought you said you guys don't talk anymore?" he eyed her suspiciously.

"We don't."

"So then how did all this come about? And why am I just now finding out about this?"

"He's in town. I couldn't say no."

"Kyra, I know you're not talking to me about going out to dinner with your ex-boyfriend. Seriously," Cincere laughed in an attempt to disguise his anger, but Kyra could see it written all over his face.

"Yeah? And? I don't see what the big deal is. We're just friends," she said.

"Yeah, and you're about to be single in a minute," he threatened.

"Oh, is that right?" Kyra cranked up her attitude in defense.

"Come on, Kyra! How would you feel if I went to dinner with one of my exes? I'm pretty sure you wouldn't be happy about it!"

Kyra kept quiet, not wanting to admit she would be just as mad as he was.

"Damn Kyra . . . I thought we were so much better than this. And I'm supposed to believe you don't still have feelings for this dude? Be for real," Cincere sucked his teeth.

"I mean, of course I care about him. You have to understand Justin and I have history. We've been through a lot together." Kyra tried to put it to him gently, but Cincere rejected her explanation.

"So that was then and this is now! There's no reason for you to still be talking to him!"

"See this is why I didn't want to tell you! I knew this was how you were going to react!" she argued.

"I mean, let's be real, Kyra what's to keep you from getting some on the side? If I didn't ask how would I know? It's not like you would tell me!" he screamed.

"Whateva, Cincere, we've been together long enough! If you don't trust me by now you never will!" Kyra met his accusations with a cold hard stare.

"Of course I trust you. I just don't trust you when it comes to Justin!" he protested.

"Why are you trippin'? It's just dinner!" she whined.

"Nah, this is bullshit, and you know it," he fumed. "How do I know he won't try to make a move on you?"

"I already told you, it's not even like that!" Kyra tried to act surprised when really, that's what she hoped would happen. The probability of her and Justin sleeping together was so high she was willing to bet on it.

"So it's that easy, huh? You're just going to act like nothing ever happened, and now everything is okay?" Cincere continued in a hostile tone.

"No. I never said that," Kyra took a deep breath to contain her anger. She was two seconds away from snapping on him and he didn't even know it.

"Do you still love him? It's okay. You can be honest." Cincere blocked her from moving.

"Cincere, I don't have time to argue with you!" Kyra tried to push him but he didn't move an inch. When she tried to pass him again, Cincere pulled her in.

"Tell him I said you're not going and that's that!" he demanded.

"I said let me go!" Kyra snatched her arm back. The look she gave told him he better back off.

"You know what? Fuck it." Cincere threw his hands up in defeat as he retreated to the other side of the living room. "Go ahead. The way I see it, you're either already cheating on me or you're about to. All I know is I'm not sticking around for when you do."

"And what the hell is *that* supposed to mean?" Kyra put one hand on her hip and proceeded to work her neck.

"Go to dinner with him and find out. Just don't expect me to be sitting here waiting for you when you get back," Cincere lowered his tone, but Kyra could still see the anger burning in his eyes.

"Look, I'm done talkin' about this. It's not like I need your permission. I already told him I'm goin', so I'm goin'," she added.

"Then go!" Cincere pointed toward the door. He wasn't about to chase after her, and he had too much pride to start blowing up her cell phone. It didn't matter how much he loved Kyra, there was nothing he could do to keep her from leaving him if she wanted to. As hard as it was, Cincere knew he had to let her go.

Kyra left in a rush to meet Justin at the address he texted her earlier that day. It was a spontaneous, last minute meeting but she wouldn't miss it for the world. They had been sending flirty texts back and forth since exchanging numbers earlier that week, and she was curious to see where their date would lead.

The moment Kyra stepped foot in the Coco Bistro she didn't give her argument with Cincere a second thought. Nestled inside an old coconut grove under a canopy of palm trees and white lights, the Coco Bistro was one of Justin's favorite restaurants, and she could see why. Most people couldn't even get in without a reservation, but as soon as Kyra told the hostess who she came to see, she was seated right away.

"Hey, sorry I'm late! I got here as fast as I could," Kyra lit up when she saw Justin was already there waiting for her.

"Don't worry about it! Glad you could make it!" Justin stood to greet her. "Wow. Let me just say you look *amazing*." He stepped back to appreciate her effort.

"Thank you." Kyra twirled around so he could get the full effect. One compliment from Justin was worth a 1,000 compliments from anyone else. No one had the power to make him feel like he did.

"Come! Have a seat!" Justin pulled her chair out for her, and Kyra gladly accepted. She gazed at him in pure admiration as she watched him take his place across the table. Something as simple as having dinner with him seemed so surreal.

"I'll be honest, I was worried you might not show after the way you ran off on me the other day," Justin started off with a joke, but Kyra didn't laugh. She shielded her eyes with her hand, totally mortified that he would call her out.

"Justin, I am *so* sorry. I hope you don't think it was anythin' personal.

It's just. . . I-" Kyra rushed to apologize, but Justin wouldn't let her.

"It's cool. No need to explain. All that matters is that we're here now – together."

"Good! Because I am happy to see you! It's been a long time. . ." Kyra smiled back at him. The feel of his hand over hers put her at ease.

"Too long. How have you been?" Justin studied her intently.

"I been a'ight I guess." Kyra sighed as she placed her napkin on her lap.

"Just all right?" he asked.

"Oh, you know the usual. How about you? What have you been up to these days?"

Kyra avoided his question by posing a couple questions of her own. She didn't want to admit that even though she took a few college courses online she only did it to appease her mother. Or that at 23 her sense of direction was no better than it was when she was 17.

"Well, I work for my father now." Justin let her know he had been welcomed into the fold however he didn't say it in a boastful way. Kyra seemed more excited by the news than he was.

"How's that going?" she asked.

"It's been going pretty well, actually. We just locked in a deal for a new resort in Cabo," he announced.

"Look at you!" Kyra applauded his accomplishments.

"Yup construction is set to start on in a couple months. Everybody's been talking about it. This new hotel is slated to be one of the most luxurious in the world," he shared.

"That's great. I can't wait to see it when it's done," Kyra was all smiles. She was so happy for him, she thought her heart might burst.

"Good evening and welcome to the Coco Bistro. My name is Bernard and I will be your server this evening. Can I get you started with something to drink? We have several fine wines to choose from." Just as their conversation was getting good, an older gentleman with a curly Monopoly mustache offered to take their order.

"I'll take a Heineken." Justin handed over his menu.

"And for you my lady," Bernard turned to her with his pen ready.

"I'll have a glass of Moscato, please," Kyra put on her most polite voice.

"Very well," the waiter scribbled a note before going on. "Would you two be interested in hearing our specials tonight? Tonight, we are featuring our shrimp skewers grilled to perfection, and served with a hot and spicy dipping sauce. We also have seared scallops, presented atop a fresh mango slaw, and for desert, we have a slice of our famous coconut pie. All of which are made from scratch using only the finest ingredients. All of which are very, very good."

Kyra took another moment to ponder the menu. Everything sounded so good it made it hard to choose.

"Can I have the filet mignon with a side of the creamed spinach?" Justin put in his order first.

"And how would you like that cooked?" asked the server.

"Well done."

"And for you, miss?" Bernard turned back to Kyra.

"I'd like an order of your lobster tacos." Once their order was complete, their waiter gave them their privacy.

During the course of their meal, Justin and Kyra had the luxury of enjoying good food and conversation. Kyra worried it might be weird at first, but they hadn't missed a beat. Although she and Justin had grown, their connection hadn't aged a bit.

Kyra was so intrigued by Justin, she could sit and listen to him talk all day. She loved hearing about all the places he visited and all the beautiful things he had seen and experienced. Justin had been very candid about his life; everything from his college years to his goals for the future. There was just one thing he forgot to mention: his status.

"So. . . Justin. . . May I ask what brings you back to Prince Paul? After all this time . . . Why now?" Kyra tucked her hair behind her ear, trying to be cute. The lighting was just right and from the moment they locked eyes, the mood was set.

Justin licked his lips in a way that said he was hungry for something that wasn't on the menu and the lust in his eyes made it hard for Kyra to restrain herself. She tried to focus, but it was hard not to fantasize about the incredible make-up sex they were bound to have. As far as Kyra was concerned, Justin could get it anytime, anywhere.

"Well, I don't know if you've heard . . . but . . . I'm getting married." Justin held his breath awaiting her reaction. The look on Kyra's face said she was absolutely stunned.

"Get out of here!" Kyra laughed it off like a bad joke but when her chest started to tighten, she worried she might suffocate.

"Nope, I'm for real," Justin laughed nervously.

"Oh. . ." Kyra smiled to hide how disappointed she was but the eyes never lie. She was crushed to find out that not only was Justin marrying someone else, he actually seemed happy about it.

"Sorry. I hope you're not mad at me. I just wanted to be the first one to tell you. You know. Unlike last time," Justin stumbled through their awkward moment. He saw her sudden lapse into silence as cause for concern.

"No! No! That's great! Congratulations!" Kyra gave him one of those weak hugs. She wanted to be happy for him. She just couldn't.

As much as Kyra tried to downplay her feelings for him, she was dying inside. It was as though her heart had already stopped beating and she was just . . . there. The past five years without him were hard enough. She couldn't begin to imagine what it was going to be like spending the rest of her life without him.

"So you promise you're not mad?" Justin double-checked.

"*No!* Why would I be mad?" Kyra played it off like she wasn't hurt. She lost the courage to tell him how miserable she had been without him. It was pointless. Her feelings were irrelevant.

"Thanks a lot, Kyra. That means a lot coming from you." Justin seemed relieved, like a weight had been lifted off his shoulders. But for Kyra, it was the opposite. She downed the rest of her wine in one gulp and signaled for another, stronger drink.

"So! When is the wedding?" Kyra perked up after a shot of Patron.

"In about six weeks," Justin made it sound like he was excited, but the deep breath he took made her question whether he was ready. His wedding was weeks away and yet he was so nervous it might as well have been tomorrow.

"What's her name?" Kyra didn't even really care to know the answer, but she still had to ask.

"Her name is Eden," Justin cracked a smile, making Kyra sick with envy. She didn't touch another piece of her food after that. One word was all it took to ruin her appetite. Three bites into her dessert and Kyra was forced to push away her plate.

"Lucky girl. . ." Kyra traced the rim of her glass with her fingertip as her mind began to wander. The only thing she knew about Eden was her name, and she already didn't like her.

"Nah, I'd say I'm the lucky one," Justin gushed. Listening to him talk about his fiancé had Kyra seriously contemplating leaving. Not only had he stabbed her in the heart, he was turning the knife.

"Eden. . . That's a pretty name. I'm sure she's a very pretty girl." Kyra analyzed Justin for an indication of how attractive she was. How much did he really care about her? And most importantly, how long could he remain faithful?

"Yes, she is. I love her very much," Justin professed his love without thinking, but Kyra still didn't want to believe him. A part of her still wanted to believe he was The One. She wanted him to love her but it was becoming quite clear as the night went on that what she wanted didn't matter.

"So, uh . . . How's the love life?" Justin exhaled, more than happy to shift the focus off him.

"*Well* . . . since you asked, his name is Cincere," Kyra threw her relationship back at him, but her satisfaction was short-lived. *At least I had a boyfriend,* she worried. Flashbacks from their argument had her feeling foolish.

"Have you guys been together for a long time?" Justin dropped his napkin.

"It'll be two years in April," Kyra estimated.

"Sounds serious," Justin polished off the rest of his beer. It shouldn't bother him that she had a boyfriend - but it did.

"It is," Kyra made sure to rub it in but Justin did a much better job at hiding his feelings.

"You know my engagement party is coming up. You guys should come," he said.

"Yeah right, your family hates me!" Kyra balked at the invitation.

"They don't hate you. They just don't know you," he explained.

"How is your family anyway?" Kyra played with her fork.

"Everybody's doing fine. Quentin and Angel are getting ready to welcome their second child - a boy. Look." Justin pulled out his wallet to show her pictures of his 2-year-old niece and an ultrasound picture of what would be his nephew. It touched Kyra to see Justin as such a loving uncle. However, it saddened her to know that soon he would be showing off pictures of his own kids.

"Ha! That's crazy! Although, I can't say I'm that surprised," Kyra commented on the fact that out of all the couples from high school, Angel and Quentin were the only one who stood the test of time. Everyone knew they were going to get married and be together forever, even back then. And, even though they were no longer friends, Kyra was happy for them. Quentin and Angel seemed to have found the kind of love everyone wished for.

"How about you, do you have any kids?" Kyra held her breath waiting for him to answer.

"No. Not yet . . . Do you?" Justin looked just as nervous.

"*Hell no!*" The look on Kyra's face was classic. They both started laughing.

"How's your momma doing?" Justin glanced up at her while signing the bill.

"She's doing fine. You know her and Matthew got married."

"Really?" Justin was astonished.

"Yeah, their anniversary just passed not that long ago. They've been together goin' on five years now," she added.

"Damn. Has it really been that long?"

Kyra simply nodded.

When it finally came time for them to leave, Justin promised that another five years wouldn't pass before they saw each other again, but she wasn't so sure she believed him. It was going to take awhile for her to accept that things had changed between them, and that they really were "just friends." On the long car ride home, Kyra came to the realization that there was no going back to the way they used to be. Nothing would ever be the same again and neither would she.

CHAPTER 5

"I should've known it was you." Meeka shifted her weight when she opened the door, a clear sign she had an attitude.

"Hey, can I call you right back? Okay. . . Bye." Meeka ended the call she was on to console her friend, who looked like she was on the brink of crying, and said goodbye to what had otherwise been a peaceful afternoon.

"What happened this time?" Meeka let out an exaggerated sigh on her way to the living room.

Finding a visibly distraught Kyra on the other side of the door wasn't much of a surprise. She had known another visit was coming.

"Just so you know, I'm about to start charging you for all these little therapy sessions we've been having lately," she chuckled.

"Sorry, but I really need to talk to you. It's important. It's about Justin," Kyra started to explain when Meeka cut her off.

"*Oh my God,* can we please talk about something other than Justin for once?" she groaned like she was dying a slow and painful death. "Every other word out of your mouth is 'Justin this' or 'Justin that'. I never even met him and I'm already getting tired of hearing about him." Meeka was just playing but the look on Kyra's face told her she wasn't in a joking mood. The sadness in her eyes was no laughing matter, and suddenly, Meeka wasn't laughing anymore.

"Sike, you know I'm just playing with you. I could tell something's been bothering you. What's been up?" Meeka prompted her to start.

"Well you remember how I told you Justin invited me to dinner?"

"Oh yeah, I've been meaning to ask you if you talked to him since then."

"Yeah, I talked to him," Kyra grumbled.

"So? How did it go?" Meeka cracked a smile in anticipation of a good story, but unfortunately, Kyra didn't have one.

"Terrible! All this time I've been hopin' maybe we can work things out and get back together, when come to find out, he's already *engaged*!" After holding back for so long, Kyra let the tears flow. Just because she had a boyfriend, that didn't mean it hurt any less. Knowing that there was absolutely no way her and Justin could ever get back together was a tough pill to swallow, but it seemed like Kyra was the only one having a hard time doing so. She didn't want to give up on the love they once shared, but it seemed as though he had already given up on her. Kyra had been replaced.

"No way. . . Did you really just say Justin is getting *married*?" It took Meeka a moment to process the information. She was just as shocked as Kyra was when she first found out, if not more.

"In six weeks…" Kyra trailed off in disbelief. Six weeks didn't seem like very long at all when she thought about it.

"*Damn!* He liked it *and* he put a ring on it!" Meeka put her hand to her mouth in an attempt to eat her words, but it was impossible to take them back. She didn't mean to instigate, but the comment came out before she could give it much thought.

"Oh, Meeka, what am I gonna do?" Kyra turned baby-like as she writhed about. "Justin is gettin' married. It's been almost a week and Cincere still isn't talkin' to me," she complained.

"Well, did you at least tell him you were sorry?" Meeka asked.

"You think I didn't try that already?" Kyra snapped.

"Give it some time. You know how guys are. Maybe he just needs his space," Meeka added.

"I don't know, Meeka. I've never seen him this mad before. It's like he can't even stand to look at me. And when he does. . ." Kyra got so upset she couldn't finish her sentence. The loving, doting, Cincere she knew was gone, and it was going to take a lot more than an apology to get him back.

"The way he looks at me. . . It's like he hates me." Kyra hung her head in shame. Just being in the same room as Cincere was enough to make her feel uncomfortable. Everything about his presence was intimidating. He just wasn't the same.

"Oh, come on now Kyra. I'm sure Cincere doesn't *hate* you! It's just you gotta understand his feelings are hurt. I doubt he would be this upset if he didn't care about you," Meeka tried to rationalize the situation, but Kyra was too emotional to comprehend.

"Well he certainly doesn't act like it," she continued. "I couldn't keep his hands off me a few days ago and now I can't even get him to sleep in our bed," Kyra sniffled. Seconds later, more tears streamed down her cheeks.

"I just feel so fuckin' stupid! I should have never gone to dinner with him!"

Kyra vented while Meeka listened. An "I told you so" had no place in their conversation.

"I mean, at least now you know. You can stop beating yourself up about it wondering what might have happened, what might have been," Meeka said. "I mean, Kyra, really? What did you hope to get out of it? You're lucky Cincere is even talking to you," she noted.

"I guess you're right," Kyra's sadness escaped in a sigh. She couldn't even get mad at Meeka for telling the truth. All she could do was accept it.

"I don't know what I expected to be honest. It's been so long. I should've known he would find someone else," she moped.

"I mean, Kyra it *has* been five years. Things change. *People* change. That doesn't mean you guys can't still be friends," Meeka reasoned.

"But you don't understand! I don't want to be his *friend* Meeka!" Kyra wailed as though she were truly wounded. Meeka tried to make it sound as if she was getting a good deal, but in Kyra's eyes platonic friendship was unacceptable. She wanted all of him or nothing.

"And I already know what you're going to say," Kyra held her hand up. "I know I need to get over him . . . but it's like for some reason I can't," she sighed. "It's just everythin' ended so suddenly. We never even really got to talk about what happened. I think that's why it still bothers me. I need answers. Closure . . . Something. . . Not this!" her anger flared.

"He's getting married to another woman in six weeks, Kyra, how much more closure do you need?" Meeka asked.

"Gee, thanks, Meeka! You always know what to say," Kyra laced her compliment with sarcasm. "Thanks for throwin' it in my face!" she huffed.

"I'm just saying! There's no sense in dwelling on the past when you can't do anything to change it! You'll only drive yourself crazy!" Meeka argued.

"But I just don't get it. It doesn't make any sense! If he doesn't care about me then why would he go out of his way to see me? He could've come, dropped off my ID, and left it at that. Why didn't he? Like you said it's been five years so what's the point?" It didn't take Meeka long to come to her own conclusion about Justin, but for Kyra it wasn't that easy. She couldn't help but question his motives in hopes they were in her favor. Because even though Justin claimed to have moved on, his eyes told a different story.

"I don't know, Kyra, I'm starting to think maybe you're reading too much into this. Maybe you just need to let it go," Meeka commented.

"You know, I almost wish he hadn't told me. I'm startin' to wish Justin never even came back to Prince Paul in the first place!" Kyra hurried to catch the tears forming along the rims of her eyes.

"Well would you rather he lie to you or tell the truth?" Meeka asked what seemed like an easy question.

"I don't know. Honestly, I don't know what to think anymore," Kyra's admission came with a troubled sigh. There was still so much emotion pent up inside of her she felt like she could explode at any moment.

"Don't worry, hon. Things are going to get better."

"Ugh! Why does shit like this always have to happen to me? Why me?" Kyra sobbed, her voice hoarse from crying. "I swear! I'm startin' to think I'm cursed!"

"No. You're just dramatic," Meeka corrected.

"Seriously, nothin' ever goes the way I want it to! Nothin' ever turns out right! This is not the way my life is supposed to be!" Kyra's temper died down to a whimper.

"Then it's up to you to change it," Meeka took a moment to let her message sink in. "Look, Kyra, I know how much you love Justin. I know how much he means to you, but life is too short to stress over any man. I don't care who he is or what he's got," she explained.

"I wish it was that easy, Meeka, but when it comes to Justin, it's not. Had it not been for our exes tryin' to break us up, we would still be together. I just know it."

"At least that's what you would like to think," Meeka interrupted her daydream. "There's no real way to know for sure."

"But don't you think me runnin' into him that day at the marketplace was a sign? That's where we first met! Think about it. What are the odds we would run into each other there of *all* places? I'm convinced it was fate that brought us there that day - not circumstance. Don't you see, Meeka? There was a reason we were both at the same place at the same time. We were meant to find each other!" All of a sudden, the feelings Kyra felt when she first laid eyes on him came rushing back.

"You know, Kyra, one thing I've learned from my past relationships is that sometimes you will fall in love with someone who won't always love you back. You can't force it. If it's meant to be, it will be," Meeka advised.

"He said he wants to see me again before he leaves, but I don't know if that is such a good idea." Kyra sounded even more nervous than before. Seeing Justin seemed to do more harm than good, and after what happened the first time, Kyra wasn't so sure she was willing to try again. She didn't need to go making things any worse with Cincere, and being around Justin would serve as another painful reminder that he wasn't hers anymore.

"Uh, Uh, Kyra, you know they say there's a special place in hell for women who cheat with married men!" Meeka scolded her as if she already knew what she was thinking.

"He's not married . . . yet," Kyra schemed.

"Maybe. . . But say you do hook up with him while he's here. Then what? Do you think really he's going to leave her? And, even if he does, could you trust him?" Meeka posed the kind of questions Kyra didn't want to answer. "I think its best you just leave it alone. Forget Justin."

"Can you believe that after all that, he actually had the nerve to ask me if I wanted to come to his *engagement party*?" Kyra huffed.

"Oh, girl, I know you were pissed!" Meeka laughed.

"Hell yeah I was mad! You damn right," Kyra snorted.

"I know you're not really going to go. . . Are you?" Meeka wondered aloud.

"Now why would you ask me that?" Kyra dismissed Meeka with a look. Barely able to stomach the thought of Justin being intimate with someone else, she definitely couldn't imagine having a front row seat at his PDA-fest.

"That's okay. I'll just tell him I already have plans that day. It's not like I *have* to go. . . I mean, I thought about it, but after talkin' it over with you I think I need to stop worryin' so much about Justin and focus on my relationship with Cincere." Kyra took a deep breath thinking of all the damage she had done to her relationship. Other than saying sorry, she didn't know how to fix it, or if it could even be fixed. For all she knew, she was already single.

"I don't know girl, sounds to me like you need a drink," Meeka changed the topic.

"More like I need a break," Kyra mumbled.

"What are you talking about you need a break - a break from what?" Meeka giggled.

"My life," Kyra's answer was plain.

"Hey, you know what? We should go out tonight! What do you say? You down for a girls' night out?" Meeka perked up, but the solemn expression on Kyra's face didn't change.

"I'm good. I don't really do the club scene like that no more." Kyra was reluctant to go, and for good reason. After all the violence that transpired surrounding nightclubs in The Chi, just the thought of partying made her ill. Breaking news broadcasts and grisly tales of murder invaded her dreams every so often. She hadn't so much as stepped foot in a club since she left Chicago, and that was in 2007.

"Aw! I don't want to hear it," Meeka dismissed Kyra's refusal with a lazy shoo of her hand. "Now go put on something cute," she ordered. "You're coming out with me tonight."

CHAPTER 6

That night, Meeka introduced Kyra to a hopping spot called Bongos. Kyra had never heard of it, but apparently, she was the only one. It had only been open a couple months, but Bongos was gaining quite the reputation as the place to be and be seen for locals and tourists alike. A nightclub and restaurant all-in-one, Bongos was known for hitting capacity well before midnight.

The crowd was hype even for a weeknight, so Kyra could only imagine what it must be like on the weekend. It was only Tuesday, and Bongos was full of beautiful women and men on the prowl. Kyra and Meeka could barely take two steps without someone grabbing at them or trying to get their attention. Heads turned wherever they went.

Meeka kept her outfit simple with a pair of turquoise short-shorts, a white, low-cut top, and some nude wedges. With flawless skin like hers, she was killing the competition. Her kinky twists were half-up, half-down. Traces of light brown weave were added for color.

Kyra stood out from the other women in a form-fitting red dress. The tight little number accentuated her curves and the crocheted material covered only what was necessary, leaving her sides exposed. Her freak em' dress was so sexy, just stepping out of the house was likely to cause an accident.

After squeezing their way through to the lounge area, the girls were lucky enough to snag a table just as it was opening up. Kyra and Meeka settled into their cozy spot by the bar, more than ready to unwind and let loose. It seemed whenever the two of them got together the laughs kept coming. And so did the drinks.

"You gotta do one more," Meeka cheered Kyra on by beating on the table. She filled their shot glasses until they overflowed.

"I don't think I can do another one!" Kyra pushed the glass away, but Meeka pushed it right back toward her.

"*Oh, come on!* Yes you can!" she pouted.

"*No!* I can't!" Kyra waved her hand as though it were a white flag.

"Uh-uh! You better not be chickening out on me!" Meeka picked up the bottle and shook the gold liquid left inside. "Don't you waste this good liquor, girl! We still have some left!" she said.

"Uh-Uh! No more shots for me!" Kyra slid her chair back. They were more than half way through a fifth of 1800, split between the two of them. One more shot could easily take her from being tipsy to flat-out drunk.

"Oh give it here!" Meeka snatched back the shot, held it up, and tossed it back like it was nothing. Unable to speak, she slammed the empty glass down when she finished.

"*Ah-ha,* that's what you get!" Kyra pointed and laughed. Meeka tried to act all tough about it at first, but she was still coughing and patting her chest, as if that could somehow alleviate the burning sensation.

"Oh my God, that was *so* funny! I should've got a picture!" Kyra struggled to breathe. Minutes passed, and the two of them were still laughing.

"Oh my God, no," Meeka covered her face just in case. Her reaction was priceless.

"It's cool. I ain't even gonna do you like that," Kyra's laughter ended in a sigh. It was the first time that night that she was able to appreciate her surroundings; the thump of the music, the fast-paced dancing, and the smell of fried food wafting through the air. Red light bulbs dangled from the ceiling, giving the club a more exclusive, underground feel. Reggae and Hip-Hop meshed well together and the dancefloor stayed packed as proof. The DJ hadn't let her down yet.

"Man! I can't even remember the last time I had this much fun!" her admission came with a smile, but before Meeka could reply, one of the shot girls stopped by with a bottle of champagne.

"Hi, ladies, good evening and welcome to Bongos!" she greeted them with a great big smile while Kyra and Meeka communicated their confusion from across the table.

"Oh, wait. There must be a mistake. We didn't order this," Kyra spoke up first.

"This bottle is free of charge - a gift from the gentleman in VIP." The waitress popped the cork anyway. She didn't bother to mention who sent it and why. The mystery deepened when Kyra discovered there was a note attached. The message read *Meet me in VIP;* however her secret admirer failed to sign his name.

"What's it say?" Meeka leaned over the table, trying to be nosey.

"Nothing important," Kyra crumbled up the note to throw it away. She wrote it off as nothing at first, but in her search for its sender, a man in black came to her attention. He hadn't said one word to her, and yet he managed to make his presence known.

There had to be hundreds of men in the club that night, but unlike them, he conducted himself like a boss. Kyra admired his calm in such a hectic atmosphere, as if he didn't have a care in the world. He sat back, watching the scene unfold from the shadows, while puffing on a fat cigar. Smoking wasn't even allowed in the club, yet security didn't seem bothered by it. No one said a word to him.

"Hey, this stuff is pretty good!" Meeka smacked her lips for taste. She read the label on the back before setting it in the ice bucket.

"Don't look. But I think it's from that guy. Over there," Kyra nodded in his direction. She could still feel him watching her every move from behind his sunglasses, but that didn't make her feel anymore compelled to speak. If he had something to say he would have to come to her.

"Who? Him?" Meeka twisted around in her seat to see who Kyra was talking about.

"I said *don't* look!" Kyra put her head down. "Can you be any more obvious?" she hissed.

"You think we should go say thank you?" Meeka turned to Kyra, who sucked her teeth at the notion. She didn't come out looking to meet somebody, and she was in no mood to be harassed and followed around for the rest of the night by some creep.

"Are you crazy? As soon as you let them buy you a drink they think you owe 'em something," Kyra complained.

"Excuse me? *Hello?* Can I get some service over here?" Kyra raised her hand, but between all the noise and the fact that everyone was so busy, no one noticed.

"Kyra, what are you doing?" Meeka jumped up and grabbed her left arm.

"I'm sendin' it back," Kyra raised her right hand instead.

"If you don't sit your ass down," Meeka scolded her for being stubborn, but it didn't make much of a difference. "Why you gotta be so mean?" she chuckled.

"I am not bein' mean," Kyra gasped. "How one minute you gonna tell me I need to do right by Cincere, and the next minute you're tryin' to get me to talk to some random guy?" she shrieked.

"I'm just saying. He was nice enough to send us a bottle. It wouldn't hurt to say thank you." Meeka turned salty.

"Whateva. Y*ou* can go over there. *I'm* staying my ass right here," Kyra continued, acting all prissy.

"Well, if you don't want it, you can at least give it to me." Meeka gave her a friendly little nudge.

"You don't need anythin' else to drink, Meeka," Kyra shot her a look of annoyance. She had been having a good time so far and would hate to have it ruined by having to clean up her friend's vomit at the end of the night.

"Come with me!" Meeka nudged Kyra again, harder this time. "I thought we came out to have fun!" she protested.

"I'm not goin' over there!" Kyra reiterated.

"Shh, be quiet! He's coming! He's coming!" Their bickering ended as soon as Meeka noticed the guy they were talking about making his way over. It didn't take long before he ran out of patience and decided to approach their table. Instead of sending another waitress, he took it upon himself to deliver a second bottle.

"Sup, Ma?"

Kyra's first impression of him was that he had a slick smile and a voice so deep she could barely understand what he was saying. All she knew was it sounded sexy. Everything about him was.

If Kyra had to guess, she would say he was at least six feet tall, maybe a little taller, with a head full of teeny tiny black curls, and beautiful brown skin. The way his clothes laid on his frame, Kyra could tell his body was in excellent shape. Upon closer inspection, she also noticed several tattoos peeking out around his collar.

"My *name* is *Kyra*," Kyra came back at him with all the stank-attitude she could muster, but he wouldn't leave her alone. Instead, he removed his sunglasses to reveal a gorgeous set of brown eyes and a face worthy of an ad campaign.

"My bad, I didn't mean to offend you, Kyra. It was rude of me to not introduce myself first. My name is Dominic. Nice to make your acquaintance," Dominic extended his hand, along with his friendship, but Kyra wasn't so quick to accept either one. When he didn't get the response he was looking for, Dominic redirected his attention to her friend.

"And your name, sweetheart?"

"Meeka."

Kyra rolled her eyes at Meeka's girly grin.

"You ladies look like you're having fun." Dominic rested his hand on the back of Kyra's chair, leaning forward to look at her.

"What do you want, Dominic?" Not one for games, Kyra cut straight to it. Her stare was hard and intimidating. Dominic seemed unfazed by her actions. Little did Kyra know that the fact that she was giving him such a hard time made him want her even more. Very few women had the ability to make Dominic nervous, but a woman like Kyra shook his confidence a bit. All she had to do was look at him.

"Well, the real reason I came over here was 'cause I noticed you and ya homegirl was sitting by yourselves. I figured you ladies are too pretty not to be in VIP." Dominic glanced at the reserved area, almost certain they would jump at the upgrade.

"No thank you," Kyra issued a rather satisfied smile.

"Meeka, tell your friend to stop trippin'." Dominic's delayed reaction told her he wasn't used to rejection. The word 'no' was like a foreign language to him.

"Yeah, Kyra, stop trippin'!" Meeka co-signed as expected, but Kyra was content right where she was.

"I'm good. Thanks anyway."

"A'ight. Yo, that's cool. I still had to let you know you the baddest chick in here tonight, hands down."

"And you know this!" Kyra snapped her fingers like a diva, giving him the proper dose of attitude to validate his claim.

"And feisty too," Dominic smiled.

"You know you like it," Kyra flirted back.

"Yeah. You're right. Maybe I do." Dominic stared at her for a moment with a strong desire in his eyes, and Kyra felt powerless against his wishes.

"Whateva," Kyra laughed off Dominic's advances in an effort to defuse them, but that didn't stop them from coming. When Dominic wanted something he was relentless.

"So you sure you don't want to come join me? I got more liquor at the booth. Whatever you want." Dominic lingered a little while longer, hoping he might be able to persuade her.

"Yes, I'm sure," Kyra stayed firm in her answer.

"A'ight, Yo, I'mma let y'all have y'all fun. Nice meeting you, Kyra and Meeka. You be smooth." As soon as Dominic turned to leave, something told Kyra she couldn't let him walk away.

"I like your accent... Where are you from?"

Dominic didn't get far before she reeled him back in with the question. During their conversation, she picked up on a certain swagger they didn't have back home in Chicago. His confidence bordered on cockiness, and she liked it.

"Brooklyn," Dominic was quick to answer, and more than proud to represent for his borough.

"Okay, Dominic, from Brooklyn. What do you do?" Kyra knew from the second she met Dominic that flirting with him could be dangerous. That was what made it so much fun.

"I'm a boxer," Dominic flicked the ashes from his cigar on the ground before taking another toke of some of the finest tobacco the West Indies had to offer. Kyra watched as he then took another drag, blew a cloud, and sucked it back in before speaking. The smoke in the back of his throat altered the sound of his voice.

"*Okay!* Don't get it twisted! Everybody knows the real G's come from the Chi!" Kyra was trying to play it cool, but so far she liked what she was hearing. She figured if Dominic really was a boxer like he said, he was he must've been a really good one. He had a certain air about him, and judging by the Frank Mueller on his wrist, he was a heavyweight in *and* out the ring.

"Yo, Ma, how old is you?" Dominic let out a sexy laugh.

"Old enough," Kyra sassed him as she worked her neck.

"Aw, alright, I'll let you think you runnin' things for now. But that's just 'cause I think it's cute," Dominic flashed another smile that made Kyra want to melt.

"Better act like you know," Kyra pressed her lips together at the end of her sentence. She was trying hard not to show that Dominic was having an effect on her when really he was tearing down her defenses one by one. She didn't know what it was. There was just something about him.

"Yeah, okay. Like I said. . . For now," Dominic blew more smoke out the corner of his mouth before putting the cigar out. "So what's the deal, y'all coming or what?" His question was much more urgent than before.

"Um. . . Who you think you talkin' to like that? You don't know me so please don't act like you do." Kyra didn't hesitate to check him.

"Well don't you think it's time we change that?" When Dominic waved the girls onward, Kyra looked to Meeka for advice on what she should do, but all Meeka offered was a shrug.

"Kyra, this is my partna, Rico. Rico, this is Kyra," Dominic introduced her to a dark-skinned gentleman with bug-eyes and thick dreads running down his back. Kyra pegged him as a high roller based on the designers he had on and the gold bottle in his hand.

"And this is my girl, Meeka," She piped up on behalf of her friend, who might as well have been hiding behind her.

"Hey," Meeka smiled and waved at Rico, who simply nodded in return. Rico struck Kyra as the type of guy who thought he was too cool to smile, but the way he kept staring at Meeka, she didn't have to question if he was attracted to her.

"Why you acting all shy? Don't be scared. Come sit down," Rico patted his lap, but Meeka chose the chair next to him.

Dominic and Kyra got close on the couch.

"Alright, so now that we're here go ahead and ask me anything you want to know," Dominic rested his arm, eager to hear what she had to say next.

"Okay. What brought you to Provo for starters?"

"My little sis is getting married." The look on Dominic's face said more than enough. Kyra could tell he wasn't looking forward to going, and she didn't blame him. Just the sound of the dreaded M-word was enough to make her want to gag.

"Next question. . ." Dominic took a swig straight out the bottle.

"How long are you in town?" Kyra took a sip as well.

"Not long. Just a few more weeks and then I start training for my next fight," he informed.

"Do you have a girl back home?" Kyra fished for more information, although she already assumed he probably had several women. She could tell Dominic was a bad boy just by looking at him.

"If I had a girl what makes you think I would be over here talking to you?" he countered.

"Just makin' sure," she smiled.

"And how about you, Miss Kyra, you're way too fine to be single. I know somebody done wifed you up by now." Dominic didn't even attempt to hide the fact he was checking her out or that he liked what he saw.

"Maybe. . . Maybe not. . ." Kyra cocked her head to the side. She couldn't stop smiling even if she wanted to. For some reason, Dominic seemed to have that effect on her.

"Damn. So it really is true. All the good ones are taken," Dominic laughed to mask his disappointment. Really, he wasn't worried either way. The fact that Kyra already had a boyfriend made him even more determined to steal her from him.

"That's what they say." His stare made her nervous. Kyra felt kind of bad for lying, but then she reminded herself that technically, she wasn't. She didn't know where things stood with Cincere and, with everything going on, she didn't want to spend the night alone.

"That's really too bad you know," Dominic scooted away from her.

"And why is that?" Kyra twisted her mouth.

"'Cause I've been told I'm a pretty good dancer," he bragged.

"Ha! You can't dance!" Kyra laughed.

"Keep it up! I know what you're thinking, but you ain't gon' be sayin' that when I twerk you out," he threatened.

"Yeah right, *cut it out!*" Kyra cracked up.

"I would show you but I wouldn't want your boyfriend to try to beat me up," Dominic threw in another sigh just to make her laugh.

"I don't know. . ." Kyra debated whether or not to brave the dancefloor. She hadn't been to the club in so long she worried she might look stupid compared to other girls.

"Come dance with me!" Dominic latched onto her and started to pull.

"No! Wait!" Kyra planted her feet, but she was no match for him. Dominic yanked her out her seat.

"That's right! Get up!" he cheered.

"Okay, but just one song!" Kyra put her finger up.

Out in the middle of the dance floor, the music made it hard for them to hear, but neither one of them needed an excuse to get close. As they moved with the music, the sexual tension between them thickened until they could no longer ignore it. So many different scenarios clouded Kyra's mind as she pushed up against him. She felt guilty just for thinking of some of the freaky things she wanted to do to Dominic.

Kyra told herself she wouldn't give in to temptation, but her feelings for Dominic were coming on strong. She wanted him and, even though she knew she was wrong, she didn't care. Everything about him turned her on, from his thick biceps to his mysterious brown eyes and lustrous black hair. He had a well-defined jaw-line and a nice set of juicy lips she *really* wanted to kiss. One look at Dominic, and Kyra didn't even have to question if the sex was good. She was sure of it.

"So what's it gonna be, Shorty? You coming with me tonight?" Dominic gripped her waist.

"I'll think about it." Kyra proceeded to seduce him with her dance.

"Move it faster," Dominic's orders came in the form of a whisper, and Kyra didn't hesitate to fulfill his request. When "Turn on the Lights" started to play, she made sure to put in work. Kyra bit her bottom lip as she wound her hips, which only did more to excite him. One look in his eyes and she knew he was ready.

The temperature in the room kept rising until the mirrors started to fog, and Kyra could feel her own body temperature doing the same. Fanning herself did nothing to help. It was almost too hot to breathe.

"Hey, I need to go cool down for a second!" Kyra ran off before Dominic had a chance to react. She joined the rest of the patrons that spilled out onto the patio in an attempt to catch her breath.

"Hey, where are you going?" Dominic wasn't far behind.

"Sorry, but it is *so* hot in there!" Kyra sucked in all the air she could.

"You want something else to drink, some water or something?" Dominic pulled out a wad of hundreds when he made his offer, but Kyra wasn't impressed.

"No. That's okay. I'm about to go get Meeka. I'm ready to go home."

Kyra was on her way back inside when Dominic blocked her. "But you can't go yet. It's only one-thirty. The club don't close for at least another half hour," Dominic mentioned it casually, but the look in his eyes said he would be sad if she left.

"I know, but I'm tired. Plus, it's late," Kyra covered her yawn. For someone who used to live to stunt, she couldn't hang like she used to. Her low tolerance ranked her as a light-weight.

"So that don't mean we have to say goodbye, Shorty. What you got up after this?" Dominic whispered in her ear. A single kiss on the nape of her neck left her tingling from head to toe.

"Dominic, I can't. . ." Kyra shied away from him.

"Why can't you?" he questioned; his gaze intent.

"Because, Dominic... I already told you. I have a boyfriend," Kyra mumbled.

"*Actually,* you said 'maybe' which tells me even if you do, it can't be that deep." Dominic took another step toward her, turning up the pressure.

"Well I do and I don't need you tryin' to mess it up," Kyra shot back with a nasty look, but underneath her hard exterior, her willpower was dwindling. She couldn't believe he would go so far as to use her own words against her.

"Okay. So you have a boyfriend. Clearly, he ain't hitting it right." Dominic leaned against the railing, calm as could be.

"Dominic!" Kyra burst out laughing.

"Am I right or am I right?" Dominic was confident, like he already knew the answer.

"You are out of control right now!" Kyra laughed some more.

"Look, Kyra, I don't want you to think I'm trying to ruin your relationship 'cause that's not what I'm trying to do," he continued.

"Oh. Is that right?" Kyra folded her arms.

"Yeah, you know, given the fact we just met, I think it's important that you know I would never ask you to cheat on your boyfriend. I'm simply asking you not to cheat yourself out of the experience. That's all." Dominic stared deep into her eyes as he played with her curls. They were standing so close to each other, Kyra could feel his heartbeat as though it were in sync with her own.

"I don't know, Dominic... What if he finds out?" Kyra took a deep breath. While her heart and mind were deliberating on whether or not she should give Dominic a chance, the effects of the liquor were beginning to set in. And once that happened, there was no telling who would win.

"It's not like I'm going to tell him," he laughed.

"Yeah, but. . ." Kyra hesitated.

"I don't even see why you're so worried about him. Your boyfriend isn't here right now. I am," he said.

"I don't know about this, Dominic." Kyra released her stress in a sigh. She had been looking for some sort of an escape, and Dominic was looking like the next best thing.

"Don't worry. I promise I'm worth it," Dominic flashed that megawatt smile of his, and Kyra was blinded by his charm.

"Okay."

"Hey! Where were you? We've been looking all over for you guys." Meeka pulled Kyra into a hug the second she showed up. She and Rico hadn't left the booth all night which could help explain why they looked so bored. When Kyra and Dominic left they looked like they were engaged in an interesting conversation, but by the time they got back, they were both on their cell phones.

"Sorry, I stepped out for a minute. Everythin' straight?" Kyra asked.

"Ugh, girl, I'm starting to get a headache. Are you almost ready to get out of here?" Meeka shifted anxiously. She was more than ready to go.

"Yeah, me and Dominic were just about to leave." Kyra glanced over to see Dominic and Rico talking in hushed tones. She blushed when he winked at her.

"Wait, I know you're not about to go home with this dude. Are you?" Meeka questioned her in disbelief.

"Yeah, I'm thinkin' about it. Why?" Kyra challenged.

"Kyra, you barely even know him! What if he's crazy? He could be a serial killer for all you know!" Meeka panicked.

"I'm pretty sure he's not a serial killer, Meeka," Kyra laughed.

"Hey, I'm just saying. You never know. . ."

"Whateva, Meeka. You need to chill for real." Kyra sucked her teeth.

"Come on, Kyra. You know I can't just let you leave with him. We come together. We leave together. Those are the rules," Meeka cited girl code in her defense, but Kyra remained defiant. She blocked out everything Meeka was saying so that she could zoom in on Dominic as well as what he was wearing. He looked good dressed in Louie V down to his feet. She couldn't wait to see what he was working with underneath.

"What rules?" Kyra scoffed at the idea of someone telling her what to do. She had never been the type to play by the rules so she didn't know why Meeka thought she was about to start now. In her world, rules were meant to be broken. And when it came to Dominic, she planned on breaking every single one.

CHAPTER 7

With just a few minutes left until the lights came on, Rico and Meeka followed Kyra and Dominic out to beat the crowd. Meeka didn't say another word to Kyra about leaving with Dominic, and they left it at that. Meeka didn't look too happy with her decision to go home with him, but Kyra was okay with that. It wasn't her decision to make.

"Hey, heads up!" Dominic threw Kyra the keys to his Porsche once they reached the parking lot.

"Who said I was drivin'?" Kyra stopped dead in her tracks.

"Kyra, hurry up!" Meeka called out from the backseat of a taxi, but when Dominic wrapped his arms around her, Kyra waved her off with a promise to call her in the morning.

"You are now." Dominic fastened his seatbelt, leaving Kyra no choice but to get behind the wheel.

"Now let's go. Where I'm taking you isn't far from here." He pointed at the road ahead as Kyra shifted into Drive. One look at him sitting next to her and something told her, her night was far from over. One look in his eyes and Kyra got the feeling her night was just beginning.

"Pull up right over there," Dominic directed her to an open parking space. After driving for miles, the two of them finally reached their destination: Treasure Bay Marina. Located on the Southside of the island, it seemed like it took them forever to get there. However, the change in scenery was well worth the drive.

One of the first things Kyra noticed was how peaceful it was. Other than the stars and the moon, the sky was remarkably clear. The salty smell of the ocean was especially strong. Rows of sailboats and million-dollar mega yachts bobbed on the surface of the bay as their flags snapped in the wind. It was fairly quiet on the docks other than the sound of water gently lapping against them.

Kyra followed Dominic down the pier until they reached a boat with the word ORION painted on the hull. Dominic climbed on board. Suddenly, Kyra didn't feel so adventurous.

"It's okay. We're not going out on the water tonight." It didn't take long for him to pick up on her hesitation. He extended his hand to help her aboard, hoping she trusted him enough to take it.

Kyra ran her hands over the soft leather seats while walking to the bow and back. She took her time examining the other features such as sun beds and a twelve-person whirlpool on the top deck while Dominic kept himself busy at the ship's main point of entry. He pecked at seven digits on the keypad before pressing the Enter key. After several failed attempts, the light finally turned green.

"After you," Kyra strolled right on in, but Dominic's eyes followed her before he did. He licked his lips as he looked her over from head to toe and back up again. The sight of her supple skin through the holes in the fabric only helped fuel his desire. Dominic grinned, just thinking about having her to himself for the evening.

Once inside, Kyra tried not to gawk at the posh quarters. She knew what it meant to be "hood rich" but she had never seen wealth of such magnitude up close. Everywhere she turned, she was met by marble and gold. A second, smaller Jacuzzi greeted her when she first walked in, along with a poker table and a fully stocked, premium bar. The TV was the size of a movie theatre screen.

But out of all those things, a built-in aquarium captured her interest. Kyra tapped on the glass and a school of colorful fish broke in every direction, stirring pebbles from the bottom. They hid amongst the bright pieces coral, while she continued to terrorize them for her own amusement.

"You like?" Dominic rested his chin on her shoulder. His hands traveled across her stomach.

"How romantic." Kyra closed her eyes and let her body relax into his.

"Wait until you see the master suite," he hinted.

"Why don't we go take a look right now?" Kyra spun around to face him. She let a single strap fall as she sashayed down the hallway with a come-hither look that commanded he follow, and Dominic wouldn't dare disobey.

Kyra stood back while he removed his watch and the rest of his jewelry. Dominic took his time, setting each piece down carefully on the dresser before finally setting his sights on her. The anticipation of what was about to happen next had her breathing heavy.

Kyra indulged in the softness of his lips as well as the gentle cradle of his hands on her breasts. Much like Dominic, his kisses were irresistible. When he went to lay her down, she didn't try to fight him.

Dominic's size had Kyra trembling beneath him. She did her best to keep quiet as he titillated her breasts with his tongue, but she couldn't contain her moaning. Dominic licked her nipples slowly, creating the most incredible sensations. His lips felt like silk against her skin.

"Dominic. . ." A deep shiver rocked her body when he disappeared under the covers. She didn't know what to think when he took her panties off with his teeth.

Dominic didn't waste any time burying his head between her legs, and did so in a way that let her know he was eager to please her. He could tell when Kyra was about to lose it, but he continued to push her, blowing on her clit before he kissed it. Feeling her legs tighten around his neck gave him the motivation to lick her into submission.

As Dominic continued feasting on her as though she were his last meal, Kyra closed her eyes and let herself enjoy it. The pleasure he brought her couldn't be measured in words which would help explain why she couldn't speak. Dominic had her clutching blankets, sheets, pillows; anything she could get her hands on. The few times he glanced up at her, he caught her pulling her hair. She let herself get lost in the moment even though she knew it wasn't going to last.

All the negative thoughts Kyra had prior to meeting Dominic were replaced by how good he had her feeling. She wasn't thinking about Justin walking down the aisle or the fact that Cincere had every right to leave her for what she was doing. None of that seemed to matter at the moment. Kyra was in heaven. And if it wasn't heaven, then Dominic had convinced her she was pretty damn close.

CHAPTER 8

Dehydrated and exhausted, Kyra returned home from her wild night of partying late the next day. She crept in expecting to hear the TV or music playing at the very least, but it was quiet - almost too quiet. She wandered from room to room only to find that each one was empty. Cincere was gone by the time she got there, but her relief was only temporary. She had a long list of missed calls from him, along with a text message from Meeka asking if she made it home okay. And while she might not like it, Kyra knew she would have to answer to him eventually.

In dire need of a shower, Kyra quickly disposed of her dress on her way to the bathroom. Her goal was to get rid of any other evidence that could possibly link her to Dominic, but as Kyra passed the mirror she barely recognized the woman staring back at her. She was covered in guilt. It was going to take a lot more than soap and hot water to wash away her shame.

Memories of last night were fuzzy at best. The only thing Kyra remembered was waking up to the sound of seagulls crying out. The brisk chill that accompanies dawn filled her lungs and the splendor of the sunrise cast a faint glow around the cabin. Not that she could appreciate it. Extremely hungover, her eyes were sensitive to light to the point where she could barely open them and the constant swaying of the boat wasn't doing much to help the liquor sitting on her stomach. Leaning over the edge of the bed, she just knew she was going to throw up.

But as Kyra lay there trying to regroup, she had a revelation. She didn't own a boat. Nor did she know anyone who did. Kyra woke up with no idea where she was or how she got there. Her clothes were scattered throughout the room.

Dominic was still asleep when she slipped away, but waking up in his bed was awkward enough. And while Dominic certainly wasn't ugly, much like their moment, Kyra's feelings for him were short-lived. As soon as her buzz wore off, her attraction to him wore off with it. Once she got what she wanted she didn't want anything to do with him.

Sleeping with Dominic was a mistake she would never make twice. Out of respect for Cincere and their relationship, Kyra swore to never see Dominic again - which shouldn't be too hard considering he was a tourist. She could rest assured that one of her problems would solve itself.

Still, Kyra was smart enough to know that no relationship was perfect, and hers was no exception. Even though she didn't have it in her to come right out and confess to Cincere about what she had done, last night let her know she couldn't keep avoiding the real issue. And that was her feelings for Justin.

It wasn't like she had any real feelings for Dominic. She certainly didn't care about him more than she cared about Cincere - or Justin for that matter. And she for damn sure didn't trust him. Kyra wasn't even sure she really even liked Dominic that much.

Once Kyra had the chance to sober up, she came to the conclusion that the *only* reason she slept with Dominic was to feel better about Justin getting married. Unfortunately for her, it did the complete opposite. The pleasure Dominic provided was replaced by remorse in the morning. Her conscience was eating her alive.

Hours passed. The TV was all Kyra had for light as she sat alone in the living room, waiting for Cincere to return. One of the stations was airing re-runs of *Martin*, but Kyra wasn't really watching it. The cleverest punchlines hadn't drawn a single laugh from her. Her sense of regret seemed to build every hour Cincere wasn't there.

"Hey. . ." Kyra's greeting matched the way she was feeling. The sound of Cincere's keys had her on high alert, but the moment he finally walked through the door was even more nerve-racking than the last. She had been trying to come up with what she going to say the entire time he was gone, and yet nothing sounded good enough.

"Hey." Cincere flicked the light switch on his way to the kitchen. "You're going to hurt your eyes like that," he warned.

"I didn't know you had to work today." Kyra leaned against the doorframe, trying to feel him out, but Cincere wasn't giving her much to go on. It had been a tense couple of days since their big fight and Kyra was sure her disappearing act didn't do much to help the situation.

Cincere acted as though nothing was wrong, scrutinizing the contents of the fridge like he often did and whistling a happy tune. Cincere already had his suspicions about her cheating on him, but rather than confront her about them, he ignored her altogether. He was quite talented actually. He could go hours, sometimes even days, without saying a word.

"Yeah well it sure beats sitting at home waiting on you."

The whistling stopped when he peered over the door at her. Even the slightest glance from him was scathing.

"Nice to see you finally decided to show up." Cincere snatched a Vitamin Water off the shelf and slammed the door.

"Cincere, can we please talk about this?" Kyra followed him back to the living room.

"I don't know, Kyra. Are you sure you're ready to hear what I have to say?" Cincere popped the top and took a sip. "I've been trying to call you all morning, but your phone kept going straight to voicemail . . ." He left his comment open and waited for her to fill him in. "In all our years together, I've never known you to turn your phone off for any reason," he added.

"Sorry, my phone died," Kyra mumbled what sounded like the sorriest excuse in the book. That part of her story was true - even if he didn't believe it.

"Where you were last night?" Cincere's tone much was more aggressive than before, and his stare just as invasive.

"I wasn't with Justin if that's what you're gettin' at." Kyra let her hand fall off her hip.

"Then where the hell were you? When I left this morning your ass still wasn't back yet," he noted.

"I was with Meeka," Kyra asserted. "We went to go check out this new spot over on Provo. I forget what it's called. . ."

"So you mean to tell me you went to the club? And you didn't even say anything?" Cincere interrupted. "I hope you had fun."

"Call and ask her if you don't believe me!" Kyra burst with desperation. She knew Meeka would probably chew her out for getting her involved, but she didn't know what else to tell him. The truth wasn't even an option.

"I had a little too much to drink, and I didn't think it was safe to drive so I figured it was best if I stayed the night at her place," Kyra lied, hoping Meeka would cover for her.

"So she doesn't have a phone?" Cincere glared at her from the other side of the room. "I was worried about you when you didn't come home."

"Baby, I'm sorry. I wasn't thinkin'. . ." Kyra was at his side in seconds, but Cincere kept his distance.

"Clearly!" he blew up at her without warning. "God, Kyra how can you be so fucking inconsiderate! You could have at least called me!" he yelled.

"I said I'm sorry! What else do you want me to do?" Kyra could feel her composure withering. Her apology was genuine, and yet it was as though everything she said was meaningless.

"That's the thing, Kyra! You're *not* sorry! You knew you were wrong, but you did it anyway!" When Cincere came at her screaming, Kyra felt a wave of guilt wash over her. He was right – even if she didn't want to admit it.

"Look, Cincere, I'm not here to point fingers. I'm not tryin' to argue." Kyra cleared her throat. She could barely look him in the eye.

"I don't know what else you expect me to say, Kyra. It's not like what I say holds any weight with you. I'd just be wasting my time." Cincere shrugged her off, but Kyra refused to let it go.

"Is that what you think this is? A waste of time?" she choked.

"I'm just going off what you're showing me. And right now, it sure seems that way," he admitted.

"Cincere, you know that's not true. . . I love you," Kyra squeaked.

"Do you?" Cincere shot her a sideways glance.

"Of course I do. . ." Kyra spoke to him in a gentle tone.

"I don't know about you, Kyra. You've been acting different ever since. . ." Cincere looked away without finishing his sentence. She took his heavy breathing as a sure sign of his vexation.

"Ever since what?" Kyra studied him with furrowed brow.

"Never mind," Cincere let out a stress-filled sigh as he rubbed the back of his neck. There was no backing out of their argument. Kyra wouldn't let him.

"Ever since *what* Cincere," she got up in his face.

"Why are you even asking me this? You don't care what I think. No matter what I say you're still going to do what you want to do. Who am I to stop you?" Cincere was gruff in his answer.

"But I do care about you, Cincere. That's why I'm here. I'm tryin' to make things right. I want to make this work. . . " Kyra argued through her tears. Her emotions were raw whereas Cincere seemed to have shut his off completely.

"Cincere, you have to know I'm sorry. I didn't mean to hurt you."

Cincere didn't look moved.

"Yeah, well you did." The look he gave her cut deep.

"I know, baby, and I'm sorry." Cincere let his guard down long enough for Kyra infiltrate. "Do you think you'll ever be able to forgive me?" Kyra cried into his chest. It was going to take her awhile to forgive herself so she could only imagine how long it might take him.

"I honestly don't know, Kyra. I really don't," Cincere sighed upon sitting down. It took him forever just to answer.

"Tell me how I can make it up to you." Kyra put on the most sensual whisper. Her hand rested conveniently on his thigh.

"Let me make it better. Tell me what to do." Kyra began to kiss Cincere slowly and delicately. What started out as a kiss quickly escalated to something much more serious. Cincere's hands were all over her in his attempt to take control and dominate, but Kyra had him beat when she fell to her knees, working quickly to unzip his jeans.

"Damn, baby. . ." Cincere hissed when he felt her grip him with her lips. His body lifted off the cushions as he watched her swallow every inch. Each time she went down the tip touched the back of her throat.

Cincere kept a firm grip on her curls to assist her in deep-throating, but he couldn't keep his eyes open long enough to watch her do it. Just the sound of her sucking and spitting on him, combined with the feeling of her big, soft lips had him breathing hard. Her hands explored the deep ridges in his chest.

Kyra gauged his grunts for approval. She could always tell when Cincere was about to cum by the way his legs stiffened up. When his toes curled, she incorporated more tongue until he did.

"Now do you accept my apology?" Kyra finished up with a single kiss near his bellybutton. By the time she was done with him, Cincere could barely move.

"Apology accepted," Cincere answered her with a satisfied smile. He had yet to open his eyes.

"Listen, baby I know you had a long day. I'm sure you want to relax. Why don't you let me run you a bath?"

Kyra took it upon herself to run his water. As they waited for the tub to fill up, she took her time undressing him, making sure to remove each article carefully.

"There you go, baby. How's that?" Kyra helped him in and waited for him to get situated. She sat on the edge for a moment stroking the back of his head.

"Thanks, Babe," Cincere gazed at her with love in his eyes.

"You're welcome, baby." Kyra feigned a smile in return. She was able to breathe again after the tension lifted, but all of her worrying wore her out. She was ready to turn in for the night, but the grip Cincere had on her hand said he wouldn't allow it.

"Uh-Uh! I know you don't think you're getting off that easy!" Cincere yanked her back so fast Kyra might as well have been chained to the tub.

"What are you doin'? Ah! Cincere," Kyra hollered when he pulled her in with him. Her clothes were soaked and there was no saving her hair.

"Mmm, hmm, I got you now!" Cincere pulled her in for a kiss. Kyra wanted to be mad at him, but all she could do was laugh.

"Oh my God, look at my hair!" Kyra splashed him in the face, but that didn't stop him from laughing. Cincere was cracking up in between lots and lots of kisses.

Kyra got rid of her jeans in seconds, while Cincere volunteered to take off her shirt. They couldn't get her clothes off fast enough.

"I love you, Kyra," Cincere whispered in her ear as he positioned her just how he wanted her. Once Kyra was free, she helped guide him inside of her.

"I love you, too, baby," Kyra gave him a kiss on the cheek for encouragement.

"Promise me you'll never leave me?" Cincere pressed his forehead against hers. "Promise me we'll always be together," he breathed.

Kyra put her finger up to silence him before replacing it with her lips. One look in his eyes and all her guilt came rushing back. She had never seen Cincere so vulnerable. And while Kyra knew better than to make a promise she couldn't keep, she could no longer deny him.

"I promise."

CHAPTER 9

Even though Justin promised to keep in touch with Kyra, she didn't really expect him to. So when she got a random text from him asking her if she wanted to meet up for lunch, she was conflicted about what to do. After having just patched things up with Cincere a few nights ago, Kyra couldn't afford to jeopardize her relationship for a second time, but when it came to Justin, she couldn't help herself. Just when Kyra thought she was over him for good, Justin found his way back into her life again.

As for Justin, the week just started, and he already couldn't stand the thought of being cooped up in the office. The mountain of paperwork on his desk seemed to be growing by the minute. Unfortunately, the same could not be said for his desire to do it. As soon as Kyra texted him back, Justin told his secretary to cancel the rest of his appointments and set out to enjoy the rest of his day. When it came to Kyra, everything else could wait.

It was so nice out, Justin decided to drop the top on his newest toy; a silver Aston Martin Volante. The tops of the palm trees swayed in the light breeze as he sped past the other cars on the street. Too bad the wind wasn't strong enough to bring him any relief from the heat. The sun illuminated the spellbinding hues of turquoise in the water and there wasn't a single cloud in the sky.

As Justin drove toward the heart of Regent Village, the premier shopping plaza on Providenciales, he started to question whether he should have skipped out of work early. But, the second he saw Kyra, he knew he had made the right decision. Standing next to one of the water fountains, Kyra had on a long, royal blue maxi dress which flaunted her figure, along with a pair of gold chain Gladiator sandals and matching gold accessories; all of which complimented her skin tone. One day in the sun and she looked like a bronzed goddess.

"*Hey!*" Kyra opened her arms for a hug and Justin was more than happy to give her one. She had her curls pulled up off her neck, which helped accentuate her face, along with that smile Justin loved to see.

"Thanks for agreeing to meet me here on such short notice." Justin smiled back, completely captivated by her beauty. One look in her eyes and he was under her spell.

"It's cool. I'm glad you hit me up." Kyra made it sound like she didn't drop everything she was doing the second she saw his name come up. No one would've ever guessed she got showered and dressed in under thirty minutes.

"Yeah, you know, I hadn't heard from you since we went to dinner so I figured I'd check up on you and see how you were doing." Justin started down the walkway, past the meticulously well kept gardens and other businesses.

"That was very thoughtful of you." Kyra looked away bashfully. Just knowing he still thought about her was enough to make her blush.

"You know, Kyra, just because I'm getting married doesn't mean we have to stop talking."

"Actually, that's *exactly* what it means," Kyra laughed half-heartedly as Justin opened the door to the restaurant he picked. The maitre d' seated them underneath one of the big umbrellas outside and gave them each their menus.

"Thanks again for coming. I've just been feeling so bogged down between work and the wedding. " Justin went on. "It's nice to be able to get away for a little bit." He flashed a smile to hide his stress. Unsure whether she should ask him about it, Kyra nodded and smiled anyway.

"Speaking of weddings. . ." Justin cleared his throat. "Have you given any thought as to whether or not you're coming to my engagement party?"

Kyra paused; surprised he would even bring it up again.

"Yeah . . . About that. . ." Kyra winced at the thought of being in the same room as the girl he wanted to marry. "I don't think I'll be able to make it."

"What? Why not?" Justin looked shocked, if not a little saddened by her response.

"Hmm, I don't know. Let's see. . ." Kyra tapped her finger on her chin. "For one, I'm sure your parents would throw a fit! Oh. And then there's the fact that I'm your *ex-girlfriend*!"

"Yeah, but that was years ago. It's not like we're still messing around." Justin grabbed a breadstick out the basket. It bothered Kyra that he could be so nonchalant about something that was tearing her apart.

"Still. . . I'm sure your fiancé wouldn't appreciate me being there," Kyra remarked.

"It'll be fine!" Justin laughed. "Besides, it's my engagement party, too," he added.

"My answer is still no."

"Kyra, I don't expect you to understand why I'm asking you to do this, but just hear me out. This is a really big deal for me, and it would really mean a lot to me to know I have your blessing. I know it might not make sense, but it won't feel right without you there." Everything about Justin was gentle from his words to his caress, but the longer Kyra listened to him, the more upset she got. As much as Kyra loved Justin, when it came to him marrying Eden, she couldn't respect his feelings. She wanted to stand up and scream, *"This is some bullshit!"* but, "I'll have to check with work and see," sounded much more appropriate in a public setting.

"See, look at that! You know everything there is to know about me, and I don't even know where you work." Justin positioned himself so that he was comfortable.

"I'm a waitress over at Havana's." Kyra reached for her water to help her swallow the lump in her throat, but it did nothing to relieve her embarrassment. Sitting across from her was a successful businessman who went on to college and got his degree. No one could argue Justin wasn't doing big things, and yet there she was, waitressing.

"How did you get stuck doing that?" Justin held back his laugh. He didn't mean to offend Kyra. It was just hard to imagine her doing anything that involved her possibly breaking a nail. "I thought you worked at that one boutique. . ." he racked his brain trying to remember the name of it.

"Your guess is as good as mine," Kyra's unhappiness leaked as a sigh. She had to have asked herself that same question at least a thousand times. "Slow money is better than no money I guess," she mumbled.

"Well I still think you should try and come," Justin stuck his head in the menu.

"I'll see what I can do." Kyra said whatever she had to in order to pacify him. Justin getting married was the last thing she wanted to hear about, talk about, or think about. But as much as much as Kyra didn't want to go, the last thing she wanted to do was let him down. And then there was Cincere . . .

Kyra and Justin spent the next two hours dining on French food and fine wine at one of the sidewalk cafés. They watched the world go by, completely wrapped up in each other's conversation. Afterward, the two of them continued their stroll down Ocean's Row; known for all the big-name businesses and designer boutiques.

"Justin? Can I ask you somethin'?" Kyra shielded her eyes from the sun. They had to have covered almost every topic imaginable, but there was still one question weighing on her mind.

"Sure. Go ahead." Justin stared straight ahead; his pace slow and steady. He was in no hurry for their time to end.

"Why did you invite me out here today?" Kyra stopped abruptly.

"What do you mean? I already told you why." Justin tried to keep walking, but the look on her face said he better not take another step.

"Yeah, but I mean, I'm sure you didn't come all the way down here to talk about the weather. I want to know the real reason why." Kyra held her breath, waiting for him to say something, anything that might give her hope that one day they would be together again. If Justin had any love left for her then Kyra needed to know right away.

"Okay," Justin took a deep breath to start. "The real reason I called you is because the other night, when we were at dinner I noticed you didn't say much about yourself. It kind of left me wondering. . . How are you? Really?"

"I'm fine. Why do you ask?" Kyra fidgeted under his scrutiny. The fact that she was sweating had little to do with the temperature, and everything to do with the way he was looking at her.

"I mean, we're friends right? I'm allowed to be concerned. Just because we're not together anymore doesn't mean I want to see you unhappy, Kyra." The deep creases in his forehead backed up his claim. Justin established eye contact, but Kyra wouldn't look at him for more than a few seconds at a time. "Are you happy?" he asked.

"Yes, I'm happy. Why wouldn't I be?" Kyra laughed off his

question.

"Okay, this time I'm going to ask you again and I want you to tell the truth," Justin laughed because he she was lying.

"Whateva!" Kyra pushed him in a playful way. "While you talkin', I could be askin' you the same thing. Are you sure you're really ready to get *married?*" she teased.

"Yeah, I'm sure. I mean, you fall in love, get married, and have kids. That's what you're supposed to do, right?" Justin showed his stress.

"Remember when we used to talk about getting married?" Kyra reminisced aloud. They were only teenagers at the time, but they had it all planned out. They already knew what colors they would use and who they were going to invite. They even had a couple baby names picked out just in case.

Kyra was looking forward to building a life with Justin once they graduated from the academy, but their fairytale ended when he followed her to Chicago. Their love story was just another casualty of the city's well-publicized gun problem, and the streets weren't at all forgiving.

"Yeah, I remember," Justin chuckled. The fact that he was soon to be a married man became very real in that moment and his nerves spiked suddenly. In exactly 37 days, he would be tied to Eden . . . forever. "Funny how life has its way of working out, huh?" he commented.

"I know right. Now look at us. We're all grown up," Kyra smiled. Even though they were way too young to be talking about marriage back then, she still had faith that one day it would happen.

"Can you believe my engagement party is in less than a week and I still haven't found a suit?"

Kyra could tell Justin was in deep thought as he admired the beige suit on display in the window of a suit shop.

"You want to go take a look?"

"Nah," Justin waved off her suggestion.

"Come on. Let's see what they have," Kyra tugged at him like a little kid and, of course, Justin gave in. A small bell chime hanging above the door announced their entrance, and a man in a blue dress shirt greeted them. The shop was laid out very nicely but she and Justin were the only customers in the store.

"Mr. Hartwell! How are ya?" The salesman extended his hand. He treated Justin with a certain familiarity that said he either already knew him or he knew *of* him.

"Doing well, thanks for asking." Justin continued to roam as they talked, looking at different ties and whatnot.

"My name is Thomas, and I will be more than happy to help you. May I ask what brings you in today?" Thomas followed behind them while they browsed, offering additional information as requested.

"See, I'm getting married, and next week-"

"Congratulations!" Thomas clapped his hands together as he rejoiced in the news. "You two must be so excited!"

Kyra nearly dropped a pair of cufflinks when she realized he was referring to her. She looked at Justin, waiting for him to correct him. When he didn't, she kept quiet and waited for the awkward moment to pass.

"I think I want to try this on." Justin picked out a unique white jacket with black piping and a pair of black pants by Hugo Boss, as well as a pale blue summer suit from their summer collection.

"Okay, well why don't we get you measured up first, and then we can pull a few more pieces and see what works," Thomas said.

"Sounds good," Justin took off his burnt orange blazer and gave it to

Kyra to hold.

Kyra exhaled as the salesman measured the width of his shoulders and then down just past his wrist. The whole time she wished it was her who got to come up behind him, and reach her arms around the fullest past of his chest. She wanted to be the one to run the tape from the bottom of his neck all the way down until he told her to stop.

"Is that long enough?" Thomas looked up for his approval. Justin nodded and the salesman jotted a few more notes.

In order to size the pants, he took the tape around Justin's waist, making sure to leave it just loose enough to fit a finger in between. To get the length, he measured from his waist down to his shoes.

And lastly: the inseam. Kyra was having a hard time keeping her thoughts PG-13 as she watched the tape measure start at the top of Justin's leg, right around his crotch area and go down to his ankle. They hadn't had sex in years, but she remembered what was underneath quite vividly.

Once he had the correct measurements, Justin grabbed a few dress shirts and some neck ties to try. When he disappeared into the fitting room, Kyra was tempted to follow him. After all, if she was going to help him pick out his clothes, it was only right she get to take them off.

"That suit looks great on you." Thomas gave Justin the okay sign as soon as he stepped out.

"I don't know. Kyra, what do you think? You've always been better at this than I have," Justin looked to her for advice, and it was as though once they made eye contact, neither of them could break it.

"Ah yes, it is smart to get a woman's opinion," Thomas chimed in.

"It's okay. I kind of like this one though." Kyra held up a hanger with an all black suit attached. It was made of silk wool with black satin accents. The suit came in two pieces with a notched lapel, two buttons and two front pockets, along with one on the breast. The tag inside indicated that it was made by Tom Ford, and was nearly three times the price.

"You're right. She does have good taste," he smiled.

"Here, try this on next." Justin sighed at the suggestion. Meanwhile, Kyra's urge to shop was getting stronger. She was like a kid in a candy store looking at all the different color combinations and accessories. It didn't matter if they weren't shopping for her.

"How do I look?" Justin stepped out from behind the curtain with his hands out at his sides. He took his time admiring his look, trying to get a feel for it. He adjusted his collar like he was feeling himself and, in Kyra's opinion, he had every right to feel that way. Justin was as fine as they come, but a suit took his sexiness to a whole other level.

"That's it," she gasped. "That's the one."

CHAPTER 10

Kyra lugged the heavy wash basket all the way to the living room and set it by the couch. She inhaled the fresh scent of fabric softener as she sat down for what felt like the first time that day. She had just finished the last load of laundry and was busy folding clothes, with Cincere on the floor next to her, tapping the red and green buttons on the X-Box controller. Dinner was on the stove.

It was a typical night at home. Kyra should have been relaxing but thoughts of Justin kept her on her toes. Kyra couldn't stop thinking about him and what he said to her at lunch. And it wasn't even what he said that bothered her. It was how he said it. Beneath his lighthearted tone was this layer of protectiveness that hadn't gone away.

Justin made a habit of doing things that lead Kyra to believe he still cared about her. And with all the mixed signals he was sending, it made it harder for Kyra to interpret his true feelings, let alone figure out her own. She agreed to meet him, thinking she might be able to accept the new terms of their friendship once they talked about it. The problem was, after spending a little more time with him, Kyra wasn't sure she was ready to give up just yet.

Kyra wasn't about to be the crazy ex-girlfriend who comes busting in when the preacher asks if anyone objects, but she wasn't about to stand by and do nothing either. If Justin went through with marrying Eden he would be making the biggest mistake of his life. She just had to figure out a way to make him realize it.

Kyra had never been afraid to say how she felt, especially when it came to Justin, but she knew in order for her plan to be effective, she would have to use a more subtle approach. With their "friendship" still so fragile, Kyra had to be particularly careful when dealing with Justin. She didn't want to do anything that might make him stop talking to her altogether - like blow off his engagement party.

Kyra rolled her eyes at the thought. She didn't even want to share the same oxygen as Eden, let alone the man she loved. The only reason Kyra was even considering going was because she knew it would make Justin happy. And because while Justin tried to make it seem like she had a choice, Kyra knew the truth. Underneath it all, she and Justin were friends first. If she wanted to keep him as a friend, she would have to show support.

The first time Justin mentioned the party, Kyra thought he was doing it just to be nice. When he brought it up again, it was clear he expected her to be there. Of course, Kyra's first instinct screamed not to go, but after lunch she felt obligated to make an appearance. Either way, Kyra had a feeling she was going to regret it.

And while Kyra didn't like the idea of having to contend with another woman for his love and affection, her curiosity was growing in regards to Justin's fiancé. As much as she despised Eden's existence, Kyra was eager to size up the competition. She also wanted to let Eden know that not only did she still love Justin; she was fully prepared to fight for him.

In the middle of plotting her next move, Kyra deflated with a sigh. If she was going to go, she couldn't go alone, and while she could always ask Meeka that would defeat the purpose. Kyra already told Justin she had a boyfriend. She needed him to see her with him.

Kyra still didn't know whether she was crazy or genius for what she was about to do, but with the wedding coming up, she was willing to try anything. Bringing a girl just wouldn't have the same effect, and there was no point in going if she didn't have anyone to go with her. It was crucial she bring a date.

"Cincere." Kyra tapped him on the shoulder. His cooperation was critical to her plan's success, but getting him to agree was going to be tricky. He was the only person she knew who probably didn't want go more than her.

"One second, Babe," Cincere signaled her to stop talking. He hated to be interrupted while playing *Call of Duty*.

"Cincere, I need to talk to you." Kyra pestered him anyway.

"What is it?" Cincere pretended to be interested, but he was so absorbed by his mission, Kyra could've been trying to tell him the place was burning down. He wouldn't have realized what was going on until he smelled the smoke.

"Can you please stop playin' that game for one second and look at me?" Kyra huffed.

"Yeah, yeah go ahead. I'm listening." Cincere tapped furiously at his controller.

"Okay. Promise you won't be mad at me but I talked to Justin and . . ."

"Justin?" Cincere pressed Pause and sounds of gunfire and explosions stopped. "When was this?" He twisted around to look at her.

"The other day. . ." Kyra kept her answers vague.

"What the hell, Kyra? I thought I already told you I didn't want you seeing him." Cincere got up, threw the controller down, and cut the system off.

"I know. But Cincere, you don't understand." Kyra sighed to vent. She was growing tired of the constant bickering and the frequent headaches. It was the same thing over and over again.

"You're still in love with your ex, Kyra. I think you've made that quite clear, don't you?" Cincere shot her a nasty look, evoking her attitude.

"Did I say that?" Kyra snapped.

"No, but you didn't have to. It's pretty fucking obvious," he replied.

"Look, like I said before, there is nothin' goin' on between me and Justin. The only reason he called was to see if we wanted to come to his engagement party." Kyra continued.

"We?" Cincere had to question if he heard correctly.

"I know you probably don't want to go, but I figured. . ." Kyra stopped there, unsure whether she should go on or if she would just end up making things worse.

"Okay, Kyra. Now you're pushing it." Cincere's stale laughter did nothing to dilute his anger towards her. He was pissed, and he wanted to make sure Kyra knew it.

"Cincere, it's only for one night. I really don't see why you're makin' this such a big deal," she argued.

"Man, fuck Justin and that party! This is about my respect!" Cincere hit his chest.

"So I don't respect you now? Is that it?" Kyra kept both hands propped on her hips.

"Nah, you're right. I'm trippin'. Now that I think about it maybe I'll call up my ex and see what she's doing this weekend. Yeah, that sounds like a good idea." Cincere cut their conversation with sarcasm.

"Cincere, don't do that." Instead of yelling back at him, Kyra lowered her voice. As much as she loved Justin, she didn't want to picture Cincere with someone else.

"I mean, why not? There's nothing wrong with it, right? You do it," he snorted.

"Whateva, Cincere. Do you want to go to this party with me or not?" Kyra huffed.

"That depends. Do you want me to go?" Cincere flipped the question back on her which only added to her frustration. Her patience was wearing dangerously thin.

"Of course I want you to go or else I wouldn't have asked!" Kyra had to walk away for a minute. She was going to snap if Cincere didn't give her an answer - and soon.

"I don't know. Give me some time to think about it." When Cincere reached for the remote, Kyra blocked the TV.

"Well I need to know so I can RSVP. The party is comin' up and I need to tell him if we're comin'," she stressed.

"When is it?" Cincere stared past her.

"Saturday, I believe," Kyra played it off like she didn't know all the dates off the top of her head. It wasn't like she could just come out and say that every day they got closer to July 13th she could feel her anxiety building. She couldn't tell him that when Justin told her he was getting married he might as well have been telling her how many days she had left to live.

"Wait . . . *This* Saturday?" Cincere's eyes popped open in surprise. Kyra simply nodded.

"Alright I'll go," Cincere exhaled. "But that's only because I don't want you going by yourself." He scolded her with a wary look. "I think it's about time I met this little 'friend' of yours," he said.

"Yes! Thank you!" Kyra dangled her arms around his neck. She snuck in a quick kiss on the lips before she could let go, but Cincere didn't say anything. The serious look on his face said enough.

After they ate dinner, Kyra left it to Cincere to clean up. Once she knew they were going for sure, the next most important thing for her to do was figure out what she was wearing. Just knowing Justin was going to be there meant Kyra had to bring her "A" game. However, after sorting through the hangers, nothing really caught her eye.

Either Kyra was just being picky, or every dress she owned was too short or too tight for the occasion. And, given all the added pressure of being Justin's ex-girlfriend, she had to be extra careful about how she presented herself. She wanted to be remembered for all the right reasons.

After comparing options in the mirror, Kyra narrowed it down to a third and final dress. She already passed on the pink hi-low dress with a flowy bottom, as well as a coral peplum dress she bought from H&M. But, as she pressed the black lace against her body, Kyra couldn't help but smile. All she had to do was find the right shoes to go with it and she would be all set.

It wasn't until she was in the middle of assessing her shoe collection that Kyra began to feel any sort of excitement. She had been dreading going to Justin's engagement party ever since she found out about it, but now, she couldn't wait to strut up in there and show him what he was missing. If looking good was the best revenge, then Kyra knew the perfect way to make Justin *and* his girl jealous.

CHAPTER 11

There was a twenty-piece jazz band playing as Kyra and Cincere stepped into the Grand Ballroom of the swanky Golden Palms Hotel. They, along with over 300 other guests, were transported to an all-white wonderland that was truly dazzling upon first sight. Everything from the tablecloths to the elaborate floral arrangements that adorned them was crisp and fresh. Candelabras were placed at each of the tables. The crystals that hung from them shimmered in the light.

It was a joyous occasion; a time to celebrate love and togetherness. Kyra wasn't feeling it. She and Cincere had been there all of five minutes, and she was already tempted to turn around and go home. As if the large sign announcing Justin and Eden's engagement wasn't enough to send her running for the door, her anxiety made her feel like she was at a funeral.

In a sea of vibrant colors, Kyra was one of few women wearing black. The dress she decided on wasn't made by a big brand, but its design was the perfect balance between sexy and classy. The slip was nude in color, with a lace overlay that created the illusion she was naked underneath. The material stopped mid-way down her thigh, showing just enough leg to pique a man's curiosity. Her makeup was light so as so as to accentuate her features - not hide them - and she kept her natural curls.

Kyra had gotten all dolled up, and yet she struggled to feel confident standing next to gowns worth thousands of dollars and jewels appraised at far more. In a room full of rich people it wasn't hard to tell who was and who wasn't. Cincere stood out like a sore thumb in a pair of khaki slacks and a plain white button-up, whereas the rest of the men were decked out in their finest tuxes, discussing business and politics.

Kyra took a good look around at everyone talking, smiling, and laughing. They all seemed to be having a good ol' time, and somehow, she felt so far removed from everything that was going on. From the moment she and Cincere set foot in the room, they caught quite a few curious looks as to who they were and why they were there, but not one person bothered to introduce themselves. Thanks to Veronica, Kyra assumed most of the people there had probably heard about what happened between her and Justin. Every time she heard someone laugh, she took it personally, as though the joke were on her.

"Can I just tell you, you look fantastic?" The sound of Cincere's voice brought Kyra out of her trance. He followed up with a kiss on the lips like no one was watching. And even if they were, he didn't seem to care.

"Mmm, what was that for?" Kyra purred. Her mouth was stuck in the form of a smirk and she was slow to open her eyes afterward.

"Just because I love you," he smiled. "Now here, take this. I have a feeling you're going to need it." Cincere slipped Kyra a much appreciated glass of champagne and raised his flute. The two of them made eye contact as their glasses clinked together. Kyra nearly downed hers in one gulp.

"Oh, look. There's Justin," She tried to mask her excitement when she spotted him making his way across the room. "We should go say hello." Kyra pulled Cincere along.

"Justin! Hey!" Kyra waved to him, and Justin smiled in return. He seemed more than happy to suspend his current conversation to talk to her.

"Kyra, you came." Justin appeared to be equally shocked and pleased.

He was trying to be discreet in the way he was eyeing her dress, but Kyra could tell she had a winner.

"Wouldn't miss it," Kyra was cheesing hard.

"And who is this you brought with you?" Justin acknowledged her date indirectly, even though he was standing right there.

"This is my boyfriend, Cincere." Kyra squeezed his hand and Cincere pulled her closer, almost as if to claim his territory.

"Congratulations on your engagement, bruh. That's major." Cincere nodded. "Yes, congratulations to the both of you," Kyra pushed herself to sound upbeat, but the light in her eyes seemed to fade a little.

"Thank you. Eden and I are looking forward to finally making it official," Justin rubbed his hands in anticipation. "Matter of fact, here she comes now," his giddiness resurfaced.

"Stop the music! Stop the music!" A frail-looking man stepped up on the stage and stole the mic from the host. "Ladies and gentlemen, please allow me to introduce to you to my beautiful daughter, and the future *Mrs. Hartwell,* Ms. Eden Josephine De La Cruz!" Eden stole the spotlight the moment she entered the room. Guests broke out in dainty applause as she began her graceful descent down the Grand Staircase and the band performed with new life. Cameras flashed from every angle, and there was a group of admirers waiting for Eden at the bottom, clamoring for a moment of her time.

As Kyra watched Eden interact with her family and friends, her stomach dropped. Everyone seemed to love her - not just Justin - and it was easy to see why. A Spanish-speaking siren with curves that could kill, Eden had the kind of body a lot of women envied and most men adored. Her eyes were hypnotic pools of green that looked like they glowed, and her skin was sun-kissed. Her long brown waves were pinned to one side of her head with an iced-out hairpiece to hold the style in place. The waistline of her flowy, mint-colored dress was embellished to match.

Although she would never admit it, Kyra was intimidated by Eden. She had shown up expecting to meet someone way less attractive than her but Eden possessed the kind of natural beauty that inspired legendary poets and great works of art. Kyra examined her closely for flaws, only she couldn't find any. Even her dress was on point.

"Hi, sweetie, sorry to keep you waiting. What did I miss?" Eden had a voice that was just as smooth and sultry as her looks.

"No worries. It was well worth the wait." Kyra had to look away when Justin went in for a kiss. Whenever he addressed Eden, it was as though they were the only two people in the room. His attention never strayed.

"*Ahem,*" Kyra cleared her throat in an attempt to steal some of Justin's attention for herself. The longer he waited to introduce them, the lower her patience.

"Eden, my dear, I would like for you to meet my good friend Kyra Jones, and her boyfriend, Cincere."

"Hi." Despite Justin's enthusiasm, Eden reception was rather dry. She summed Kyra up within the first five seconds, and judging by the way she stuck her nose up in the air, she thought Kyra was beneath her. In Eden's world, guys like Cincere didn't get the time of day.

"Kyra and I used to go to high school together," Justin shared.

"Um. . . Actually . . . We used to date." Kyra jumped in to correct him. She didn't appreciate the way he downplayed their relationship. His carelessness gave her the impression that he never once even mentioned her to Eden before tonight.

"That's right. Kyra is a good girl. You be sure to treat her right," Justin said to Cincere.

"Oh, I can assure you I have no problems doing that." When Cincere flashed his arrogance, Kyra checked him with a look.

"What about you, Kyra? Are you and Cincere thinking about getting married anytime soon?" Eden lifted her eyebrows in curiosity. The couple in question turned to each other for answers, although neither was quick to volunteer.

"Maybe someday." Cincere looked to Kyra to take over. Like most men, he didn't even want to touch that topic. The word "marriage" made him sweat.

"I think right now we're just taking it one day at a time." Kyra made eye contact with Justin, if only for a split-second.

"You know, I must admit I was pretty surprised when Justin asked me to marry him. It was just *so* romantic!" Every time Eden giggled, Kyra fought the urge to roll her eyes. She hadn't even been there that long, and she was already tired of her and her happy-go-lucky attitude. Everything about Eden was irritating.

"Go ahead, darling, show them your ring." Justin took another sip of champagne and Kyra did the same. When Eden stuck out her hand, she was almost blinded. A ten carat diamond sat proudly in its center, surrounded by even more diamonds which were set into a pave platinum band.

"Wow." The word fell out of Kyra's mouth as if it were heavy on her tongue. She didn't even want to look at it, as pretty as it was. Based on the cut and clarity, Justin practically worshipped Eden. She didn't even want to know how much he paid for it.

"Yup, I had it custom-made. Just like Eden, her ring is truly one of a kind." Justin proceeded to dote on her. Anyone with eyes could see how much he loved her. He was proud to call her his.

"Sweetie, I was just telling Natalie and her husband all about our trip to Saint-Tropez," Eden changed the course of their conversation. "It was *amazing*. Justin and I spent most of our summer vacationing overseas. Well, that's when he wasn't busy with negotiations." Listening to Eden talk, Kyra began to understand why Justin never felt the need to brag. He didn't have to. She did enough bragging for the both of them.

"So, Cincere, Kyra tells me you're in the construction business. Is that true?" Justin tried to reach out to him again. Cincere acted like it pained him to speak.

"Yeah, I heard about the Lilliana project. A couple buddies of mine are working at that site. Said it's really coming out nice. You Hartwells have really outdone yourselves this time," he said.

"Thanks man. I appreciate it." Justin stuffed his hands in his pockets. "You know if you're ever looking to make a little extra cash I've got a few more projects lined up for next spring. I'm sure we could always use the help." Justin flexed with a smile. Kyra could tell Justin wasn't offering Cincere a job to be helpful or considerate even. He was the boss and Cincere was the worker. It was only right he put him in his place.

"Oh! Kyra, Cincere, before you go, I would like for you to meet my brother, Dominic. He's visiting us all the way from New York City," Eden motioned him over with the biggest smile on her face.

Where have I heard that name before . . .? Kyra kept her thoughts to herself. The name sounded vaguely familiar, but she couldn't match it to a face.

"Dominic, I'd like for you to meet Kyra Jones, Justin's friend."

"Hello, Kyra." Dominic showed off a devious grin. He was the one night stand that could cost her everything. And he was standing not even two feet from her boyfriend.

"Nice to meet you," Kyra coughed. She pretended like she was meeting Dominic for the first time, but the way he licked his lips said he knew her very well.

"My pleasure. . . I'm sure." Dominic had fun toying with her. The immature smirk he wore might as well have been permanent.

"Do you two already know each other?" Of course, the first to pick up on his behavior was Justin. He glanced at Dominic, then Kyra, and back at Dominic again.

"No, I don't believe so." Kyra warned Dominic not to say anything, and she did it with a look. Needless to say, when Dominic winked at her, it didn't have the same effect it did that night they were at the club. The thought of having actually slept with him made her quiver - and not in a good way.

"Are you kidding? How could I ever forget a face like that?" Dominic flirted with her openly.

"Dominic is it?" Cincere stepped up to put an end to it, but Kyra's relief soon turned to worry.

"And you are . . . ?" Dominic stared him down like he was one word away from losing his teeth.

"I'm Cincere, Kyra's boyfriend." Cincere stood tall, ready to defend her and their relationship.

"Justin was just telling us how he and Kyra used to go to school together," Eden wrangled the boys in.

"Oh, well, while I wish I could stay to hear all about it." Dominic's eye roll matched his sarcasm. "I was just on my way to the bar. Can I get you anything? Justin, what you drinking?"

"I'm good bro. Thank you." Justin raised his glass, which was still half-full.

"Dominic, don't you go getting drunk. This is the engagement party *not* the bachelor party." Eden teased. Everyone let out a stuffy laugh.

"Alright I'll see y'all later. Nice meeting you, Kyra." Kyra was haunted by his smile even after he was gone.

"Oh, honey, that reminds me! Guess who wants to see you?" Eden cuffed Justin by the arm and roped him in. "Kyra, Cincere, it was *so* nice to meet you. Now, if you will please excuse us. . ."

Eden ripped Justin away from them, but not before she threw Kyra a victorious smile. That was her way of telling Kyra to back off. That Justin was hers now, and that next time she saw her, she wouldn't be so nice.

As Justin and Eden were flooded with well wishes and congratulations, Kyra had a sinking feeling. That should've been her standing next to him, not Eden. But when the couple posed for pictures, neither one of them could stop smiling. The crowd cheered when they kissed.

As much as Kyra hated Eden, she had to admit she and Justin made a good-looking couple. She was the first girl to make her wonder if Justin's family was right. Maybe she wasn't worthy of somebody like him? Maybe they shouldn't be together? When it came down to it, they came from two completely different worlds, and while they didn't used to think it mattered, it did. Apparently, for people with money, it mattered a whole lot.

"See. Are you happy now? I told you nothin' is goin' on," Kyra said.

"I still don't like him." Cincere squinted in Justin's direction. His stance suggested he was ready to go after him.

"Would it kill you to be nice?" Kyra chuckled.

"I don't know and I don't want to find out." Cincere lightened the mood with a joke.

"Hey babe, I don't know about you, but I could *really* use another drink." Kyra hugged his arm while resting her head on his shoulder. The throbbing in her temples was sharp and intense.

"Tell me what you want and I'll go get it for you," he offered.

"Oh, I don't know. Surprise me." Kyra put her cheek out for him to kiss it and he did.

Kyra held her smile until she was alone. Standing there on the sidelines, watching everything go on, she couldn't help but wonder how her plan backfired so horribly. She came there with the intention of making Justin jealous, but in the end, she seemed to be the only one feeling that way.

It hurt her to the core knowing she wasn't a part of Justin's life anymore. Feeling like she was on the outside looking in, it was in that moment that Kyra realized her worst fear had already come true. Justin didn't love her anymore.

"I was hoping I might see you again."

Kyra sucked her teeth when Dominic approached her near one of the ice sculptures. He showed up so fast it was like he couldn't wait to step in.

"Oh, it's you." Kyra kept it short. Now that she could talk to him, she didn't really want to. She had no interest in getting to know Dominic or be his "friend."

"I see the way you keep looking at him. I used to look at my ex-girlfriend the same way." Dominic tilted his head. "You know you're not the only one who's had their heart broken, Kyra."

"And what do you know about heartbreak, Dominic?" Kyra pushed away from him and the familiar way he touched her. "I bet you don't know the first thing about love and relationships," she commented.

"I know a thing or two."

Kyra locked eyes with him. "Listen, Dominic, what happened that night on the boat was a mistake! Cincere and I have been goin' through a bit of a rough patch which may have led me to do or say some things I shouldn't have. Things that maybe made it seem as if we could be more than friends, but we can't!" she hissed.

"It's cool, Shorty. We can keep this between us. Nobody has to know," he whispered.

"Dominic, you need to chill! I am here with my boyfriend!" Kyra didn't know whether to call Dominic bold, brave, or just plain stupid. Cincere would be back any minute.

"So that's never stopped you before," he snickered.

"Yeah, well, one thing's for sure. That'll never happen again!" Kyra turned her back on him.

"What you getting your heart broken or me and you having sex?" Dominic sounded worried all of a sudden.

"Both!" Kyra threw her hands up in exasperation. She started to storm away from him, but she didn't get very far.

"By the way... That night on the boat... Did we ... ?"

"You don't remember?" Dominic looked somewhat disappointed when Kyra shook her head. Truth of the matter was she was so drunk she didn't remember what happened that night.

"Then why don't you let me remind you?" Dominic played with one of her dangly earrings, sending Kyra's heart rate through the roof.

"Look Dominic, I really don't think now is the time or place for us to be discussin' this." She swatted his hand.

"Well when else are we going to talk about it? You didn't exactly leave behind a glass slipper. No money on the nightstand, either. Come to think of it, I never even got your number." Dominic looked somewhat peeved by the fact Kyra slipped out the following morning. Usually, it was the other way around.

"That's because there is nothin' for us to talk about, Dominic. What don't you get?" Kyra snapped.

"C'mon, Ma you gotta stop and ask yourself; when was the last time you fucked with a nigga like me? Be for real." Dominic's cockiness came across in everything he did, including his smile. "I know you gotta be tired of dealing with that lame," he chuckled.

"Here's your drink, honey." Cincere slipped his arm around her waist. Kyra couldn't get the cup to her lips quick enough.

"It's cool, yo, like I said. No rush. When you're ready, you'll know where to find me. I'll leave you two to enjoy the rest of your evening." Dominic excused himself, however his dark mood hung over them long after he was gone.

"What did he say to you?" Cincere noted Kyra's vexed expression.

"Nothin'," Kyra waved him off.

"Why was he all up on you like that just now?"

"I don't know. Maybe you go should ask him." Kyra plucked the cherry out of her drink. She swiftly removed it from the stem using her teeth.

"You know what? Forget this. I'm out." Fed up with her attitude, Cincere ditched his whiskey and coke. He was in such a hurry, he never even apologized to the people he bumped into on his way out.

Kyra was just about to go after him, when suddenly, she stopped. She couldn't walk out on Justin without saying goodbye. Not again.

"Excuse me." Navigating through the crowd, Kyra tapped a woman on the shoulder, but when she turned around, she was too shocked to move. It didn't matter if they hadn't seen each other since high school. She would recognize those blue eyes anywhere.

"Kyra?" Angel seemed to share the same disbelief. The awkward silence between them was broken by shrieks and screams.

"Oh my goodness, Kyra!" Angel opened her arms for a hug.

"Angel! It's been so long since I've seen you!" Kyra rocked her from side to side.

"*Say hi Kyra!*" Angel prompted her daughter to speak, but her little girl hid behind her leg.

"Aw, are you shy?" Kyra's heart melted when she finally got a smile out of her. She even inherited the same blue eyes. "Angel, she is *too* cute! What's her name?"

"Sanaa." Angel patted her daughter's head. "She'll be three in February, but with some of the things she says, you would think she's turning 30," Angel chuckled.

"Anyway, how about you? How have you been?"

"I've been okay," Kyra drew a deep breath. "I see you and Q got another one on the way. When are you due?"

"At the end of August," Angel groaned.

"Oh that's soon!" Kyra gasped at the firmness of her stomach. For someone who still had a few weeks to go, Angel looked like she was about to pop.

"Yeah, girl, not soon enough," Angel took a deep breath. "I am *so* ready."

"Well you look great. And I *love* your hair!" Kyra complimented

Angel's new do. It had been cut short in the back with long bangs swooped across in the front, similar to how Rihanna used to rock hers way back when.

"Thanks! I just got it cut not that long ago. It was just too hot. I had to do something." Angel ran her fingers through it while they talked.

"Well, I like it. It looks good," Kyra confirmed.

"I agree." Quentin interrupting them was similar to a storm cloud rolling in. His presence changed the whole dynamic of their conversation.

"How are my babies doing?" Quentin greeted both his wife and daughter with kisses. Sanaa extended her arms to the sky so he would pick her up.

"Hey, look who's here," Angel's voice quivered, like she was in trouble just for talking to her.

"Kyra," Quentin grumbled when he looked at her.

"Quentin." Kyra's smile disappeared. She looked the other way when she rolled her eyes.

"Sanaa, why don't you and mommy go see Nana for a little bit?" Quentin was kind when speaking to his daughter. Sanaa started to cry when he set her back down however he kept his eyes locked on Kyra the entire time. "If you don't mind, I would like to have a couple words with Kyra."

"Sure. Come on Sanaa. *Say bye, Kyra, bye-bye!*"Angel used her baby-voice before switching back to the regular. "Bye, Kyra. It was good seeing you."

Quentin kept quiet until they were gone.

"You mind telling me what the hell you're doing here?" he snapped.

"I was invited." Kyra backed away slowly. She seemed to be the only one uncomfortable with him invading her personal space.

"By who?" Quentin scoffed.

"Don't worry about it."

"Stay *away* from my family, Kyra! I'm not going to say it again!" Quentin came at her through clenched teeth. The look he gave her as he walked away was just as chilling as his warning. Their encounter made her feel so unwanted and out of place, Kyra began to question why she even came. And that's when she remembered.

After a few minutes of searching, Kyra found Justin ducked off by himself. "Hey I just wanted to tell you I'm leaving."

She looked around. "Where's Eden?"

"I don't know. I'm sure she's around here somewhere." Justin stood up straight to address her. "You sure you have to go?"

"Yeah, Cincere said he's ready to leave so. . ." Kyra shrugged.

"Well, it was great having you. And by the way, people are digging the suit." Justin played with his lapels.

"Duh, you know I have good taste!" Kyra joked.

"In clothes, anyway," Justin made sure to mumble, but Kyra still heard him.

"Uh-uh, what's that supposed to mean?" she squeaked.

"I don't know. I just always pictured you with someone kind of... different," he admitted.

"What? You mean somebody like you?" Kyra shot back, paralyzing him with her honesty. The live music and conversation from the ballroom faded into the background. It was just her and him.

"Goodnight Justin." Each step she took toward the door proved to be a struggle. Unlike all the previous goodbyes, Kyra truly believed this one was final. Justin, on the other hand, refused to accept it.

Meanwhile, Dominic and Eden were tucked away in the shadows, where no one could see them, quietly observing Kyra and Justin's conversation. Her fiancé was being a little too friendly with his ex-girlfriend for Eden's liking, and her disapproval showed all over her face. Dominic could tell she was livid by the way she was breathing.

"I wouldn't let her get too close if I were you," he cautioned.

"I don't intend to." Eden growled. "Tell me everything you know about her," she ordered.

"Not much. Her name is Kyra Jones. She's from Chicago. . . That's all I know." Dominic shared what little information he could remember.

"See what you can do to distract her," Eden instructed.

"I already tried that," Dominic huffed, still irritated from earlier.

"I said I need you to *distract* her, Dominic. Not try to have sex with her." Eden scolded.

"And what do you suggest?" Dominic raised an eyebrow.

"I don't know, Dominic. Just get rid of her!"

CHAPTER 12

Three long days had passed since Justin's big engagement party and Kyra was still suffering from the side-effects. It was the middle of the afternoon. The restaurant wasn't even that busy, and she was still struggling to keep up with the tables in her section. Her mind was on everything but work.

After such an eventful weekend, Kyra was burnt out. The friendly smile she used to greet her customers was nothing more than a façade used to cover up the nausea, sleeplessness, and depression: all the common symptoms that came along with being lovesick. It wasn't like there was some magic pill she could take to alleviate the pain she was in. No doctor could help her. There was no cure.

When Kyra ran into Justin, it was as though all of her old wounds had been ripped open again. She wanted to believe that her heart would heal eventually. All she had to do was give it time. But if she hadn't gained some sense of inner peace after five years, how much longer would she need?

With Kyra's list of regrets getting longer by the day, agreeing to help Justin celebrate his engagement had to be at the top. Kyra knew from previous experience that seeing Justin with another woman was enough to classify as some form of psychological torture. Being forced to make nice with his fiancé made Kyra feel like she was being punished for every bad deed she had ever done.

She tried to move past it, but somehow every other thought brought her back to that night, along with the emotions she felt at the time. Flashbacks of Justin doting on Eden invaded every waking moment. Kyra's skin tingled with jealousy when he kissed Eden right in front of her. After seeing Eden's ring, it almost felt as though she had been forced to ingest the humungous rock and lug it with her wherever she went.

Short of breath, Kyra stopped to rest against the edge of the closest table. Functioning on just a few hours of sleep, her vision became blurred, and she felt unsteady on her feet. When her emotions began to manifest as physical aches and pains, she wasn't sure if she was about to vomit or faint.

"Hey, Diane do you think you can cover me for a few minutes?" Kyra reached out to the first person who passed her.

"Sure. It's pretty slow right now." Diane took a look around the dining room.

"Thank you." Kyra loosened her apron.

"You don't look so good. Are you going to be okay?" Diane's motherly instinct kicked in.

"Mmm, hmm," Kyra agreed to avoid any more questioning. She retreated to the area designated for employees only, however, her pace quickened the closer she got to the backdoor. When she pressed all of her weight against the metal bar, warm sunlight met her in return.

"Oh, thank God." Kyra felt relieved to find Meeka on her lunch break. After holding so much inside, she couldn't wait to sit down with her and unleash.

"Hey, what are you doing out here?" Meeka checked the time on her phone. "I thought you don't get a break for another hour?"

"I don't, but I couldn't wait." Kyra claimed a chair for herself and put her head down. "I need a minute."

"What's with you? You and Cincere get into it again?" Meeka swatted at a pesky fly trying to steal a bite of her food.

"No. Not exactly . . ." Kyra stalled. She had noticed a change in Cincere however it wasn't quite the change she had been hoping for. He treated her more like his roommate than his girlfriend.

"Then what's the problem? Are the customers getting on your nerves again?" Meeka laughed, thinking back on some of the horror stories.

"I met Eden." Still traumatized by the experience, it took all the strength she had left not to break down right there.

"Now, Kyra, *why* would you go to that party?" Meeka looked like she pitied her already. "I thought you said you weren't going to go!"

"It's not like I really wanted to!" Kyra argued. "Justin kept askin' me."

"So you guys have been hanging out a lot lately?"

"I wouldn't say all that. I've only seen him a few times since he's been home," Kyra shot down her assumptions.

"I still can't believe you went to his engagement party!" Meeka exploded. "What the hell were you thinking?"

"I wish I could tell you." Kyra got weak. When it came to love, it never was that easy.

"Why didn't you call me? I would've gone with you," Meeka said. "And *please* tell me you didn't go there by yourself." Her eyes widened with worry.

"No. I had a date," Kyra remained prideful.

"Who?" Meeka jerked her neck.

"Cincere," Kyra's voice went flat.

"You took him with you! Kyra . . ." Meeka left her mouth open. She kind of wanted to laugh, but felt like she would be wrong if she did.

"Yeah, yeah," Kyra shut down her lecture quick. Meeka was going to have to save all that for another time.

"So is she pretty?" Meeka's bluntness made Kyra cringe, but Kyra couldn't even fault her for asking. It was the number one question every girl wanted to know. As soon as a girl found out her ex had a new girlfriend she automatically rated the new girl's worthiness based on whether she was prettier than her. And for some reason, out of all the criteria they were judged upon, looks always seemed to be most important.

"She's okay I guess." Kyra's comment was accompanied by a sour look. Because while Eden might've already had the Hartwell's approval; she would never have hers.

"Ugh, I am so over you and Justin." Meeka closed the container she was eating out of and tossed it in the trash. "Whatever happened with you and that one guy from the club? What was his name?" Meeka sucked the rest of the sauce off her fingers.

"Dominic." Kyra rolled her eyes so hard they almost fell out of her head. Running into him at Justin's engagement party was quite the surprise, although she wouldn't describe it as pleasant. Feelings of shame and guilt resurfaced as soon as he did.

"Oh. You'll never guess who his sister is," she hinted.

"Wait. So he was there?" Meeka was slow to catch on.

"You know, Justin's fiancé, Eden? She's the little sister he was tellin' me about." Kyra described the disaster she had been faced with.

"No!" Meeka covered her mouth.

"Yes." Kyra nodded.

"So do you think Justin knows about you and Dominic?" Meeka whispered.

"No. But at this point, does it even matter? We're not together so it's not like he can be mad at me. Plus, if you saw how he was with Eden, you would know he clearly doesn't care about me anymore." Kyra's anger quickly dissolved into hurt.

"Not that I don't feel bad," she sighed. "I mean . . . What are the odds that the first time I have a one night stand it's with his brother-in-law?" Her expression was one of disappointment and disgust.

"Very high, apparently," Meeka tried to draw a laugh out of her, but Kyra wasn't amused. Because of Dominic, she would have to delete Justin's number from her phone altogether. All she had to do was push a button, but it wasn't that easy to erase Justin from her mind.

"Come on, Meeka you know it's only a matter of time before my name gets brought up and Justin starts askin' questions. How does that make me look?" she worried.

"Yeah, you got a point there." Meeka sucked air through her teeth.

"Did you ever hear from his one friend, Rico or whatever?" Kyra asked.

"Not really. We exchanged numbers, but he got on my nerves always asking me to send a pic."

"Ugh!" Both of the girls looked at each other and laughed. They even made a similar face.

"Alright well, let me get back up in here before Chris get to yellin'." Kyra dusted herself off. She didn't even want to think about how much trouble she would be in if she got caught.

"Okay. Just remember you can always call me if you need anything."

"I will." Kyra smiled as she was leaving. She appreciated the reminder, although part of her hoped she wouldn't have to take Meeka up on her offer.

"Hey, Kyra, I need to talk to you."

Kyra clenched her eyes shut. She was sure she was busted until she realized who the deep voice belonged to.

Justin bumped right into her.

"Hey... What are you doing here?" Kyra's laughter came as a result of her confusion. The way he came storming into the restaurant, she thought somebody owed him some money. She had never seen him look so determined.

"I came to see you. You got a minute?"

"My shift isn't over until eight." Kyra groaned, thinking about the six hours she had left. "Call me later?"

"I would, but we need to talk - now. This can't wait." Justin sounded almost irritated by her suggestion.

"Well, it looks like it's gonna have to." As Kyra went about checking on her tables, Justin followed close.

"Excuse me sir, is there a problem?" Kyra's manager joined their conversation. Chris had no reason to address Justin in such a confrontational manner, but one look at the baggy Balmains Justin was wearing and he assumed Justin was there to cause trouble.

"No problem." Justin kept a cool head. It was hard to get mad when he knew he had enough money to buy the building they were standing in. He could even have it named after him if he wanted.

"Is everything okay here?" Chris turned his next question over to Kyra.

"Yeah, we were just talking," Kyra mumbled. Customers were starting to stare.

"Sir, I cannot have you harassing my staff and disturbing my guests. I'm sorry, but I'm afraid I am going to have to ask you to leave," Chris whispered so no one else could hear.

"I'll leave. But she's coming with me." Justin grabbed her hand like it belonged to him.

"I beg your pardon?" Chris didn't understand, and Kyra looked just as confused.

"Kyra will no longer be working for your establishment effective immediately," Justin took the liberty of speaking on her behalf.

"What! Chris, don't listen to him," Kyra fought to get her hand back. She didn't know what provoked him to do it, or what was about to happen next, but Justin made it clear he wasn't leaving unless she was leaving with him. He didn't care if he had to carry her out himself.

"Go get your stuff. We're done here," Justin ordered her along despite her objections. The way he spoke to her let her know Chris wasn't in charge anymore. He was.

Kyra's manager turned to her for answers, but the look she got from Justin shut her up. She cleaned her locker out in minutes.

"Justin, what the *hell* are you doin'?" Kyra tore into him once they reached the street. "Are you fuckin' crazy? I can't just leave!" she screamed.

"I'm doing you a favor." Justin kept walking, unfazed by her tantrum.

"A favor?" Kyra glared. "Justin, you just cost me my job!" she whimpered. "Now what am I goin' to do?"

"That's because I have a better one for you." Justin turned to face her.

"What?" Kyra sniffed back her impending tears.

"You remember when we were in Chicago?" Justin leveled with her, eye to eye.

"Like I could forget." Kyra sighed.

"What happened that summer changed the both of us. But I would like to think it changed us for the better, wouldn't you?" he continued.

"Justin, what the hell are you talkin' about?" Kyra snapped out of it.

She had gotten so lost in his eyes she almost forgot why she was mad.

"I want to help you," Justin explained. "But only if you let me."

"And you really thought this was the best way to go about it?" Kyra came back at him with full-blown attitude.

"Maybe not . . . but I've been meaning to ask you this for awhile now so here it goes. . ." Justin took a deep breath. "Kyra, I want you to be my personal stylist," he announced.

"You can't be serious." Kyra put her hand to her forehead. She didn't look nearly as excited.

"Hell yeah, I'm serious! Do you know how many compliments I got on the suit you picked out?" Justin struck a pose that made her laugh. "Plus, I know fashion has always kind of been your thing. So I figured hey why not let you worry about it? I'm too busy to keep up with that kind of stuff, anyway," he said.

"But, Justin, I don't know the first thing about being a stylist," Kyra admitted.

"Don't worry. You can start with me until you build your clientele. Trust me. I know a few people who could use your help." Justin laughed a little. "It's just with me still being so new to this industry I need to make a good impression. I can't afford to let people think they can run over me. And besides, you know what I like." Justin licked his lips after he looked her over. The second he put his hand on her shoulder, Kyra soaked her panties all the way through.

"Consider this your retainer for the month." Justin pulled a thick stack of money from his pocket, and Kyra's eyes lit up. The brick of cash was bound by a mustard-colored band.

"But Justin, there is $10,000 dollars." As Kyra ran her thumb over the bills, she was overcome by the same excitement she felt when she first saw him. That was more than enough money for her to take care of some business and do something nice for herself. All her problems were solved - all but one.

"That's nothing. You'll see. That is if you're serious about this?" Justin looked up through his brow.

"Wow. You have no idea what this means to me, Justin. Thank you!" Kyra couldn't deny she was tickled by the gesture. An opportunity was the most meaningful gift Justin could ever give her.

"So it's settled then." Justin opened his car door. "If you're free tomorrow, I need you to do some personal shopping for me."

"Sure. What do you need?" Kyra stepped up, eager to serve.

"Well I have a pretty big press event coming up so if you could pick out a couple different outfits to choose from that would be great. When you're done make sure you call me, and we'll set up a time to go over everything." Justin handed over his black American Express as he ran down the instructions.

"Don't let me down, Kyra. I really need your help on this one. I need someone I can trust," he confessed.

"I won't." Kyra promised.

"Oh, and make sure you get some rest tonight. You have a busy day ahead of you tomorrow. I already recommended your services to a good friend of mine."

"Okay." Kyra perked up when he kissed her cheek. It had to be at least ninety degrees outside, but the firmness of his chest pressed against hers still gave her chills.

"Let me know if there is anything else I can do. If there's anything else you need - anything at all - don't hesitate to ask."

CHAPTER 13

"Cincere, come here!" Kyra came bursting into their apartment with several large bags weighing down each arm. Once Justin gave her permission to use his credit card, she wasted no time putting it to use. Still brimming with excitement in regards to her new position - as well as the fabulous perks that came with it - the fresh smell of retail gave her a high she didn't want to come down from. Being able to shed her work clothes for the cute silk romper she wore out of the store was symbolic of her revival, and Kyra was more than ready to embrace a life of luxury.

"You're home early." Cincere noticed the three hour difference before her new look. All the noise lured him from the bedroom, but he stopped short when he saw the living room littered with shopping bags. "What's all this?" he asked.

"I went shoppin'." Kyra said it like it was some kind of accomplishment. Tired and out of breath, she took in the mess she made with great satisfaction.

"Damn girl! Did you buy the whole store?" Cincere seemed just as anxious to find out what was inside the bags as he was to find out who was footing the bill. "Since when do we have money for all this?" His forehead scrunched with worry when he questioned one of the mile-long receipts.

"Babe, *relax,*" Kyra chuckled a bit. "Half this stuff isn't even for me," she confessed.

"Then who's it for?" Cincere grew agitated when he discovered that most of the bags contained men's clothing – none of which were his size.

"It's for work." Kyra slowly removed the Dior frames from her face and returned them to their case. Cincere let his suspicious glare speak for him.

"Baby, guess what?" Kyra bit her lip to keep from smiling too hard.

Cincere entertained her with a rather unenthused, "What?"

"Your girl got a new job!" Kyra got hype. It was hard not to be considering all the possibilities: the places she could go, the people she could meet.

"Congratulations. Where at?" Cincere was slow to react. When he opened his arms for a hug, Kyra gave him a peck on the lips instead.

"Baby, you are never goin' to believe this! I was at work today when Justin came in…." Kyra started to tell him all about it, when Cincere shut her down.

"What was Justin doing at your job?"

"He came up to the restaurant and offered me a chance to work for him," Kyra explained.

"Doing what exactly?" Cincere stepped back to assess the situation.

"I know this might sound kind of crazy but he asked me to be his stylist," she giggled.

"And you agreed?" Cincere huffed in disbelief.

"Well . . . yeah. I mean. . ." Kyra wrestled with her reply. His negative reaction made her wish she kept the good news to herself.

"But you already have a job."

Kyra rolled her eyes at the reminder. "Correction: I had a job," she mumbled.

"So you quit? Is that what you're saying?" Cincere kept poking at her with his questions. All it took was a head nod to set him off.

"What the fuck! You can't just quit your job!" Cincere came down on her hard. "Damn it, Kyra! I would have appreciated it if you had at least talked to me about it first!" he huffed some more.

"I'm sorry, baby, but I had to take it. If I didn't take this job I wouldn't have a job, period." Kyra made an effort to smooth things over, but it didn't work. Cincere was heated.

"No. You didn't have to. You wanted to! There's a difference!" he hollered.

"Whateva, Cincere! You weren't even there!" Kyra's attitude seeped through her voice.

"Take this shit back! All of it! Tell Justin we don't need him or his money!" Cincere balled up one of the shirts and stuffed it back in the bag.

"What? I can't take all this stuff back." Kyra let out a weak laugh. They were practically swimming in new merchandise. Plus, she had worked too hard to carry all them in just to turn around and carry them back out.

"I said take it back!" Cincere hurled one of the bags toward the door, scattering its contents. Kyra ducked just in time to avoid being hit.

"What the hell, Cincere? You are really fuckin' trippin' right now!" Kyra got loud. As her boyfriend, Kyra expected Cincere to offer his love and support, but he refused to give her either.

"No. The only person who's trippin' right now is you!" he yelled. "You think I'm fucking stupid, Kyra? His stylist?" His laughter was as mean as his comments.

"Damn, my bad. I thought you would've been happy for me." Kyra put one hand on her hip and let the other hang. "Do you know how much more money I'll be makin'? This will be good for the both of us!" she claimed.

"And besides, it's not like I'll be workin' for just him. I'll work for other people too. As a matter of fact, I'm scheduled to meet with a potential client tomorrow," Kyra continued. Meanwhile, Cincere stared her down as he ran his tongue along the inside of his lip.

"And you really expect me to believe you?" He eyed her with contempt. In his mind, she was already guilty.

"Oh. You don't?" Kyra scrambled to find her purse amongst the bags. She pulled out what was left of her bankroll, fanning the hundreds out for him to see, but his expression never changed.

Cincere picked up the phone.

"Um, excuse me, but . . . Who the hell are you callin'?" Kyra shifted her weight in offense. She was baffled at how Cincere could start another conversation without finishing theirs first.

"I'm calling Chris. You need to talk to him. Tell him you're sorry and you want your job back." Cincere held the phone out for her to take it. The timer started which meant it was ringing.

The pressure was on.

"Now you and I both know I'm not about to do that." Kyra put an end to the call as well as his idea. With an easy ten-grand in her pocket, she couldn't even think about going back to bi-weekly paychecks that didn't even last a full two weeks. Not even for him.

"I swear, I'm starting to think you be trying to make me mad on purpose! Like the shit is funny!" Cincere speculated out loud. "Keep thinking this shit is a fucking joke, Kyra!"

"Whateva, Cincere! I don't know what your problem is! You're always mad at me about something!" Kyra tossed the phone on the cushion. With the way he was acting, she couldn't even take him seriously.

"No. I am not *always* mad. You just do shit to piss me off!"

Kyra counted to five before she got ready to speak. "Look, Cincere this is the one thing I might actually be good at. Why you wanna take that from me? If it wasn't for Justin, I'd probably be stuck at that damn restaurant for the rest of my life. At least this is an opportunity-"

"Don't you see what's going on, Kyra?" Cincere cut her off mid-sentence. "This isn't about you. This is about Justin! This is his way of keeping you close to him!" he argued.

"Come on now, Cincere. I thought we were past this." Kyra sighed as she leaned against the back of the couch.

"Yeah, so did I," Cincere went cold as he retreated to their bedroom. Kyra tensed up when he slammed the door. An unopened bottle of wine was left on the coffee table, but Kyra didn't know whether to celebrate or drown her sorrows. Because at the end of the day, all she had to hold onto was hope for a better tomorrow.

With yesterday's drama behind her, Kyra got up early the next morning to put herself together. She knew if she was going to go around telling people she was a stylist, then it was important she look like one. Otherwise no one was going to take her advice. And although, Kyra never quite pictured herself in the position of fashion stylist, the more she thought about it, the more it started to make sense. Being thrust into her new role without any warning or preparation was a little nerve-racking to say the least, but Kyra was confident in her ability to piece together a showstopper. She had done it before and under the right conditions, she knew she could pull it off again. All the reassurance she needed was right there in the mirror.

Looking good and feeling good had always been synonymous for Kyra, but that day she stepped out feeling unstoppable. After yet another lengthy internal debate, she decided on a belted, raspberry-colored pencil skirt, with a sleeveless, cream-colored satin top, and a metallic gold Michael Kors tote to set it all off. The metallic T-strap sandals she wore were also made by Michael Kors, minus the MK monogram. Pressed for time, she finished by tying her hair up in a top knot. She would have to apply her gloss in the car.

Kyra was officially on her way to her first consultation, and yet all she could think about was how happy she was to leave Cincere and their drama at home. It hadn't even occurred to her that she was speeding until she was half-way there. When it came to her success, she wasn't about to let anyone slow her down.

After spending most of her night of arguing, Kyra was really looking forward to meeting with Justin - until she saw who he brought with him. Having Eden around always made for an awkward situation. When it came to their chemistry, it was clear she didn't mix.

Eden seemed to stare harder at her than at Justin. Kyra caught more than a few dirty looks while in the midst of discussing the season's hottest trends. It didn't surprise her at all when Eden managed to point out something wrong with each one of her selections. The opposite of Justin; Eden was rude, impatient, and nearly impossible to please.

Good thing she only had to put up with her for half an hour. Her heart was still beating a mile a minute when she pulled up at the Black Pearl Hotel around 1:30. She made her way across the lobby on her way to Suite 717, but the longer Kyra waited for someone to answer, the more anxious she became. It was then that she realized, other than the time and location Justin provided, the man on the other side was a total mystery.

"Oh, hello, you must be Kyra." An older gentleman came to greet her not long after the second knock. He was short and stocky, so much so that Kyra could see that he was balding. What little hair he had left had turned white, but the light in his eyes was bright and youthful.

"Yes, hi," Kyra smiled to hide her confusion. He was the last person she was expecting to see.

"Ah, yes. Right this way, Madam." The butler ushered her in. Kyra followed him through the opulent, two-story suite to an infinity pool outside.

"Thank you." She stopped near the water's edge, and the butler bowed before he left. Her focus was on the fine young brother, who made doing one-handed push-ups look easy. Unable to see his face from where she was standing, she could tell he was built like a God.

"Dominic." The click-clack of Kyra's heels against the pavement stopped at his head. He traced her lovely stems all the way up to the frown on her face.

"Woo-Woo," he whistled. Upon reaching two hundred, Dominic hopped up to retrieve his water bottle, lifted it to his mouth and proceeded to suck it down.

"You can save your compliments." Kyra got hot just looking at him. The fact it was 87 degrees and sunny had nothing to do with it. Dressed in nothing but a pair of white boxer shorts, the tattoos on his arms and neck were merely an extension of the artwork adorning his upper body. His sweaty chest was gleaming. His breathing started to slow.

"Oh, hi, Kyra, nice to see you, too," Dominic flashed his signature smile. Not only did he know how to identify her weaknesses, Dominic was an expert when it came to playing upon her vulnerabilities. She didn't even have to tell him she and Cincere got into it last night. It was like he already knew.

"How can I help you Dominic?" Kyra loaded her question with sarcasm. Had she known he was the person she was supposed to be meeting with, she definitely would have cancelled.

"Well, I heard you're the hottest stylist around. Is that true?" Dominic wandered over to one of the lounge chairs. Kyra opted to stand.

"Your sources would be correct," Kyra refused to smile for him. "But since when do you need a stylist, Dominic? It's not like you don't know how to dress," she said.

"I am pretty fly huh?" Dominic stroked the patch of hair on his chin.

"You a'ight," Kyra sucked her teeth at him and laughed.

"So then why did you try to play me like that at the engagement party?" Dominic got all serious.

"I didn't play you. You played yourself." Kyra snapped. "I told you what it was. You knew I had a boyfriend."

"Nah, you were trying to show out." Dominic shook his finger at her.

"Look, Dominic, I came here to work. If the only reason you hired me is because you thought you were about to get some ass, you can forget it," she warned.

"No, that's not why," he insisted. "I wanted to see you. But since you wanted to be difficult. . ." he sighed.

"Ugh. Whateva, Dominic. Just for that, I should walk out of here right now." Kyra glanced back at the suite.

"You could. But that wouldn't be smart." Dominic didn't move an inch.

"Dominic, I *really* don't have time for this." Kyra crossed her arms.

"I don't know if Justin told you or not, but my birthday is coming up next month." Dominic blotted the beads of sweat on his forehead with a towel. "I'm going to be 28 this year, and I think it's about time to start making some changes in my life - starting with my wardrobe," he explained.

"Okay, well since I'm here do you think you can you give me a general description of your style preference? Oh and I'll also need to know your sizes." Kyra leaned forward, ready to take notes.

"Well I guess you could say I like that exclusive shit. You know. I'm looking for something different, something hot. . . Something real . . . grown and *sexy* you feel me?" Dominic licked his lips in a provocative manner.

"Umm, let's try to stick to the subject, please. We're supposed to be talkin' about *fashion,* remember?" Kyra could feel her lust for him creeping up her spine. The tingling sensation between her legs was spreading throughout the rest of her body. No matter how hard she squeezed her thighs together, it couldn't be stopped.

"Yeah. . . What else did you think I was talking about?" Dominic made the slyest grin. He was the furthest thing from innocent.

"Mmm, hmm, just makin' sure," Kyra hummed. There was slight pause in conversation as she finished up on her tablet and put it away. "Alright, unless you have any questions for me I think I have everythin' I need. If not, I'll call you," she said.

"I gotta go to this stupid rehearsal dinner tomorrow, but feel free to hit me up."

Dominic handed her a check for $1,500 once inside. "Here you go. This should cover it for today."

"Thanks." Kyra quickly zipped the check away in her purse. Her next stop was the bank.

"Hey, before you go, I was also hoping you might be able to help me sort through my closet this week? I need to get rid of some stuff before I fly back to New York. If I don't, it's going to be hell when it comes time to pack," he complained.

"Sure, I can do that." Kyra agreed in hopes Dominic would finally let her leave. "Anything else?" she huffed.

"Yeah, actually, there is." Dominic moved fast in his attempt to kiss her, but Kyra knew better than to let him do it. It was already hard enough not to succumb to his passion or those delectable lips. Just one taste was dangerous.

"You love teasing me don't you?" Dominic sounded frustrated and turned on all at the same time. "When you gon' give me what I want?" Dominic caged her in. The tip of his nose grazed her ear before his lips settled on her neck.

"Uh, uh, Dominic, Nice try, but this is strictly business." Kyra grabbed him by the face and forced him to look her in the eye. Her free hand found the handle, allowing her to slip away just before their lips touched.

CHAPTER 14

It was late when Justin slipped out onto the adjoining terrace connected to his secret hideaway. Elevated high above the waterline, he stood fixated on the water below. The tide crashed against the shore and receded into the black abyss that was the ocean. The waves were illuminated by the moonlight; however, the sights and sounds of the Atlantic did little to calm him.

Justin hadn't heard from Kyra in days, but she never left his mind for more than a few minutes. It didn't seem to matter where he was, who he was with, or what he was doing. His thoughts almost always drifted to his ex. He felt bad for even thinking about cheating on Eden, but his cravings were becoming so intense he didn't know how much longer he could talk himself out of it. Too much time had passed since Justin made Kyra climb the walls, and seeing her with someone else made him question if he still held that power. There was only one way to find out.

Justin was momentarily distracted when he received an alert on his phone. He walked back inside to see he had a new text from Eden, but he didn't bother to read it. He set the phone face down on his desk as he threw back the rest of his nightcap. He didn't plan on coming home anytime soon.

* * * * *

"Congratulations on your new job, Sweetie!" Kyra's mother lifted her wineglass in celebration. After her and Kyra tapped glasses, they each took a sip.

Kyra figured Meeka's ears could use a break so she ventured over to her mother's for dinner. Working full-time kept her from stopping by to see her as often as she would have liked, but when she did, they always had plenty to talk about. The wine flowed as did their conversation.

"So, tell me more about this new job of yours. Where is it? And what are you going to be doing?" Her mother carried her smile with her all the way to the kitchen, and got started on a salad.

"What would you say if I told you I'm a stylist?" Kyra grabbed the bottle when she got up.

"And what made you decide that? You just woke up one day and said 'This is what I want to do'?" Her mother's laughter confused her. Kyra didn't know if she laughed because she thought she was incapable or because it sounded unrealistic. Either way, she was offended by how quickly her mother's surprise turned to skepticism.

"I know this might seem kind of sudden. But I mean, think about it, Mom. It's perfect! Even when I was little, I always loved playin' dress up. I've always been obsessed with clothes. Everybody who knows me knows I'm all about bein' fashionable," Kyra rambled.

"Whew, child, I remember those days!" Her mother shook her head. "You used to love trying to walk around the house in my heels. Had me scared to death you were gonna fall and break your neck!" she chuckled.

"Yeah, but I didn't." Kyra offered a stern reminder.

"I hope you don't mind me asking, but how did all this come about? Don't you need some kind of schooling to do something like that?" Her mother munched on one of the carrots she was cutting up.

"Yes. . . No . . . I don't know! All I know is that the restaurant will be there. This opportunity won't," Kyra reasoned.

"Have you put any thought into going back to school? I can't imagine you'll really make that much money around here. Especially without a degree."

"I have. But for now I'll just have to learn as I go," Kyra admitted. "Plus, I already have two clients. Not too bad for somebody who is just startin' out right?" Kyra could feel her confidence dwindling by the second. The one thing she wanted most from her mother was her validation but she had yet to receive it.

"I don't know, Kyra. Something doesn't sound right." Her mom scooped up the little carrot pieces and added them to the bowl of lettuce. "Are you sure it's not some kind of scam?"

"Just trust me on this. I know this is what I'm meant to do." Kyra locked eyes with her mother.

"Well! You seem like you already have it all figured out. I don't know why you are even asking me." Her mother sliced through the rest of the vegetables so fast she almost cut a finger off.

"Because you're my mother... *Hello!*" Kyra spoke with her hands.

"I already told you what I thought. Just because it might not have been the answer you wanted, doesn't mean it's changed any," she huffed.

"But don't you want me to be happy?" Kyra pouted. The hard look on her mother's face softened instantly.

"Of course, I want you to be happy, Kyra . . . And if this is what it takes, then hey, I say go for it." Her mother sighed when she added the cucumber to the mix. "I'm sure it'll be pretty easy for you. It's not like you've ever had a problem spending other people's money," she joked.

"Ha, ha, you would be surprised." Kyra let out a dry laugh. Her mother sucked her teeth.

"Really, Kyra, how hard could it be?" she challenged.

"Well, just know it's a *little* more complicated than you think."

"How so?" Her mother glanced up while slicing a tomato.

"Because I'll be workin' for Justin."

The steady chopping sound stopped at the end of Kyra's sentence. Her mother dropped the knife on the floor.

"Not Justin Hartwell?" All the color drained from her face. Her wide eyes captured her fright.

"Yes him." Kyra cowered, too afraid to say his name again. The way her mother placed her hands on the countertop it was as though she needed it to hold herself up.

"Kyra what the. . ."

"I know." Kyra reached for a refill only to find that the bottle was empty.

"But I thought you. . ."

"*I know,*" Kyra groaned.

"I'm not going down this road with you again, Kyra! You can if you want to, but I'm not!" Her mother came around the counter.

"Chill out! We're just friends!" Kyra explained.

"You would be smart to stay away from him altogether. You got lucky the last time. People like the Hartwells are far more dangerous than these little thugs on the street claim to be," she whispered.

"Mom, please. Don't start. . ." Kyra put her head down.

"I just don't understand. You have made *so* much progress! Why would you want to go back to that?" Her mother's voice cracked.

"Mom, you don't understand. It's not like how it was before. Things are different now. . ."

"What? Are you going to wait until somebody dies to end it? After everything you went through in Chicago I'd hate to see something similar happen here," she worried.

"What do you have against Justin? He never did anythin' to you."

Her mother shot her the craziest look.

"He broke your heart, Kyra. And he left me here to pick up the pieces just in case you forgot!"

Both women fell silent for a moment. Kyra hadn't spoken about the nights she woke up screaming, but that didn't mean she forgot. And from the looks of things, neither did her mother.

"You know he's gettin' married in a few weeks. . . " Kyra blurted out the news.

All her mother had to say was, "Oh."

"*Yeah,*" Kyra gave her confirmation and an attitude. "So like I said; for the fifty-millionth time: Justin and I are just friends. And this job is just that – a job."

"Well then you need to find another one."

"Why?" Kyra challenged her mother's orders, as usual.

"Because I can see how easy it would be for you to get wrapped up in him all over again."

"But, Mom, where else am I going to find a job that combines all my interests? At least I get to have fun. Plus, I get paid really well. And soon, I'll get to travel. Maybe I'll even meet a few celebrities. You never know," Kyra dreamed out loud.

"And you get to see Justin." Her mother added to her list. "You're so much better off without him, Kyra. You would see that if you gave yourself time to heal."

"Mom, can we please talk about somethin' else? You're killin' me right now," Kyra cringed as though she were in actual, physical pain.

"Alright, but just remember, sweetie, you're still young. You have your whole life ahead of you," she continued. "Don't you worry about Justin. You'll find love like that again. It'll come. When the time is right, it will happen," she predicted.

"Yeah, well I'm not getting' any younger here," Kyra huffed and puffed.

"Oh, sweetheart, there are other guys out there. Better guys. . . What about Cincere?"

"Ugh. What about him?" Kyra rolled her eyes; something she did far too often when thinking about him. Her mother sounded much more hopeful than she did.

"How is he? I haven't seen him in awhile."

"I really don't know and I *really* don't care," Kyra studied her nail polish for chips.

"I thought things were going pretty good for you two? What happened?"

Kyra sighed at her mother's repeated attempts to pry into her private life.

"They were. But that was before he started actin' crazy. As soon as he found out I was even talkin' to Justin, he accused me of cheatin' on him so you can imagine his reaction when I told him he offered me a job."

"Well I can understand why he would be mad. Justin isn't just your friend. He's your ex." Kyra didn't get a chance to dispute her before Matthew walked in the room.

"Hey, you," Matthew snuck up behind her mother and began massaging her shoulders. She fed him some of her homemade pasta sauce to taste.

"Mmm, that sure is good." Kyra wasn't sure whether Matthew was referring to her mother's cooking or her kisses. It was still kind of weird whenever she caught them being intimate, but overall, she couldn't complain. In all their time together, she rarely saw them argue. Matthew seemed perfect for her mother in every way.

"Oh, hey there, Kyra, how's it going?" Matthew offered her the same friendly greeting he always did.

"Good! She was just telling me all about her new job," her mother answered for her.

"Oh you got a new job? Congratulations!" Matthew lit up.

"Thank you, Matthew. At least *somebody* is happy for me." Kyra kept her eyes on her mother.

"Hey honey, I was just finishing up here. Why don't you go wash up? I'll call you when it's ready," she dismissed her husband with a kiss. She pressed pause on their conversation until he rounded the corner. When she opened her mouth again, her voice was soft and steady.

"Look, Kyra, I know how you feel. After I lost your father, I thought I would never love again, which is why I am so grateful to have met Matthew. He's helped me realize that despite all I've been through in my life, I'm stronger now because of it. There was no need for me to still be toting that baggage around with me so many years later," she testified. "You know, Kyra, not a lot of people know what it's like to love someone for all they are - and all they aren't. But at some point, you have to see it for what it is, not what you want it to be."

Kyra shifted her attention to her cell phone when it started vibrating in her pocket. She glanced at her mother and then back at the name on the screen. Justin was calling, and that $10,000 dollar retainer meant when he called, she answered.

"Excuse me. Sorry, but I have to take this." Kyra put one finger up as she pressed the phone to her ear. "Hello?" she whispered.

"Kyra, I need to talk to you," Justin declared.

"Sure. What is it?" Kyra cleared her throat. She could feel her mother staring hard. The only reason she was quiet was because she was listening.

"I'll tell you when you get here," he said.

"Okay, okay. I'm on my way." Kyra grabbed her keys. It was late and she was tired, but she was too intrigued to go home and go to sleep. If Justin said he needed her then that was all she needed to hear.

"Sorry, Mom, but I gotta go." Kyra got the side-eye when she kissed her cheek. Her mother didn't even bother to ask her where she was going. She knew who she was going to see.

"You be careful, Kyra."

CHAPTER 15

It was close to midnight when Kyra arrived on the secluded end of northern Providenciales. Justin stayed in a gated community 30 minutes away from her mother's house, but she made the drive in half the time. She was in such a rush to see him, but as soon as she got there, it took her at least ten minutes to get out the car. A thousand questions were swirling around in her head as she approached the intercom.

"What's goin' on? Is everything okay?" Kyra stormed past him without an invitation. Expecting to find him distraught and in need of comforting, all of her worrying had been for nothing. Not only did Justin appear to be perfectly healthy, his condo was clean.

"Everything's fine now." Justin revealed a manipulative grin. He knew Kyra would come through for him. She always did.

"You're lucky I don't cuss you out for blowin' up my phone like that! You made it sound like it was an emergency!" Even though she was irritated, Kyra kept her voice down. Assuming Eden would come walking through the door at any minute, it was hard to get comfortable.

"You can relax. It's just us." Justin sensed her uneasiness. She refused his offer to sit down and made sure not to touch anything. She treated his home like it was a museum.

"Nice place you have here," Kyra complimented the unobstructed ocean view, bamboo floors, and vaulted ceilings as they roamed from room to room. The short tour ended at the bar cart, where Justin proceeded to pour them each a generous amount of cognac.

"Thank you," Justin cleared his throat. "Eden's been trying to talk me into selling it."

"You don't sound like you like that idea?" Kyra scrunched her nose.

"I'm not really sure if I want to. Buying a house is a big investment," Justin brought his glass to his lips.

"And marriage isn't?" Kyra quipped.

"Eh, it's still nice to have your own." Justin hung by the window, gazing into darkness beyond.

"But it's so quiet," she complained.

"That's okay. Quiet is good sometimes. Gives you plenty of time to think about things. . ." Justin leaned against the glass.

"Like what?" Kyra's anxiety peaked under his stare.

"Like you, us. . ." His eyes continued to travel.

"Can we please not talk about that?" Kyra looked away for as long as possible, which wasn't long at all. She was convinced Justin left his shirt unbuttoned to distract her. Her hormones were on fire.

"I miss your company. That's all," he shrugged.

"Isn't that what you have a fiancé for?" Kyra's comment let him know she wasn't happy with their current situation, and to her surprise, the feelings were mutual.

"You're right. I do. I just always imagined it would be you," he admitted.

"Okay. You know what, Justin? That's it. I'm goin' home." Kyra blew him off, but the pain in his eyes kept her anchored.

"I know you've probably been wondering why I didn't come back right away. . ." Justin sighed.

"Hey, you said it yourself. The past is the past. I suggest we leave it there," Kyra warning was cold, with a stare to match.

"It wasn't because I didn't want to. And it for *damn* sure wasn't because I don't love you. . . I couldn't," he stressed.

"That's okay, Justin, you don't need to explain yourself to me." Kyra lightened up her tone.

"Yes, I do. I need you to know how I feel. I need you to know the truth," Justin panted. "I never blamed you for what happened in Chicago. It wasn't you who pulled the trigger," he whispered.

"Then why do I feel just as guilty?" Kyra's voice cracked.

"Listen, what happened that night was both our fault. I should've been upfront with you from the beginning and told you who I was. I should have never gave you a reason to question my love for you." Justin looked as regretful as he sounded.

"Whateva. Why are we even talkin' about this right now? I have a boyfriend, and you're engaged! End of story!" Kyra argued.

"Is it?" Justin broke his silence just before she reached the door.

"What did you just say?" Kyra looked over her shoulder.

"Who says this has to be the end?" Justin walked up on her, smooth and slow, like a predator approaching its prey. "Just because we're not together, that doesn't mean I don't care about you. . . You do know that right?"

Kyra closed her eyes and sighed. The smell of his cologne still did something to her. His touch still held the power to make her melt.

"What's the matter? Is it because you know there's still something between us?" he pressed.

"Um, in case you forgot, there is no 'us'. You ain't my man no more." Kyra looked him up and down.

"Look, Kyra I know I hurt you, but I was young then. I'm a man now," he declared.

"Trust, I can see that," she muttered.

"So you mean to tell me you can honestly sit here, look me in the eye, and tell me you don't feel anything? Nothing. . . Nothing at all," Justin stepped up to challenge her.

"Yes." Kyra straightened up. She didn't so much as blink, but Justin could tell she was lying.

"So is that why you reacted the way you did when you saw me at the marketplace?" he scoffed.

"I don't know what you're talkin' about," Kyra lied.

"Yes you do! Because you feel it, too, don't you?" Justin moved in close. "I felt it then and I feel it right now as we're standing here. I've felt it getting stronger every day ever since the day I met you, Kyra."

"Justin, you and I both know this is never gonna work. How are we ever gonna see each other? It was hard enough as it was and now look!" she whimpered.

"I don't know, but I'm willing to do whatever it takes. Nothing can keep us apart. Not if I can help it." Justin brushed her hair out of her face. "We might not be able to see each other every day like we used to. It'll be hard but we can make it work. I don't know how, but we'll figure something out. If anybody can do it, we can."

"Justin, you don't understand. I can't lose you again." Her vision blurred just thinking about it.

"Look at all we've been through. Compared to that, this is nothing," Justin smiled, if only slightly.

"Look, Kyra, I'm just as scared as you. What makes you think I would ever want to be without you?" Justin grazed her lips with his, taking a moment to savor the taste.

"Uh-Uh, This isn't right, Justin." Kyra pushed him off, but Justin came back for more. He dispelled her concerns with the deepest, most passionate kiss either of them ever experienced. One kiss was all it took to spark the undying passion that lay dormant for the past five years. One kiss and she was ready to surrender completely.

"Shh. . . Come here." Justin wanted Kyra so bad they didn't even make it to the bed. He bent her over the edge of the dining room table, announcing his arrival with a kiss on her shoulder blade. In his hurry, he hoisted up her skirt and pulled her panties to the side. He wasn't playing any games.

"Damn baby. . ." The pressure of him entering her triggered a sense of euphoria for the both of them. Still showering her with kisses, Justin reached around to massage her clit, using his fingers to stimulate her with her own warm lubricant. Kyra was exceptionally wet.

"Stop running," Justin gripped her hips as he dipped further into uncharted territory. Turned on by his aggression, her cries grew even louder.

"Justin!" Kyra arched her back to its breaking point, repeating his name as though he were the greatest. Her first orgasm left her too weak to stand so Justin picked her up and set her on the surface. He was so eager to be inside her again he grabbed her by the ankle and pulled her to the edge. Kyra wasn't going anywhere.

"I know you ain't tapping out already," Justin whispered in her ear while he hit it. His hands roamed over her thighs and breasts.

"No," Kyra dug her nails into his forearms. Each stroke was even more phenomenal than she remembered.

"Oh, you like that, huh?" Justin couldn't resist talking shit. All Kyra could do was nod in agreement.

"Justin?" Kyra buried her face in his neck.

"Yes, baby?" He breathed heavily, still working hard to please her.

"I've wanted this so bad, baby, you just don't know," Kyra gasped in reaction to an unexpected thrust.

"Tell me how bad you want it," Justin continued kissing and licking on her flesh. Her moans escalated to shameless screams as he dug deeper inside her.

"Oh, Justin, I missed you so much!" Kyra clung to him as one move seamlessly blended into the next, and Justin wasn't scared to test her flexibility. He pushed her legs back until she thought they were going to break. For a moment, it was almost as though pleasure and pain felt the same.

"Show me how much you missed me," Tired and out of breath, Justin encouraged Kyra to take charge and mount him. When he sat up to meet her, she threw her head back toward the ceiling.

"Tell me you love me," Kyra wrapped her legs around his midsection and squeezed. Justin gripped her shoulders while she rode him slow.

"I love you, Kyra." Another kiss and Kyra didn't even think to question him. Their future remained uncertain, but the night was theirs, and no one could take that from them. After that night, there was no more holding back.

CHAPTER 16

"Daddy!" Eden turned into a little girl the moment she looked through the peephole. It wasn't like her father to show up unannounced, but that didn't mean she was any less happy to see him. She ran into his arms.

"You should've called and told me you were coming!" Eden greeted him with a kiss on both cheeks however her smile was quickly waning. After repeated attempts to move their conversation to the kitchen, her father was still stationed by the door.

"To what do I owe this pleasant surprise?" Eden giggled nervously. Her father's eyes were as hard as the marble floor they were standing on, but it was his silence that was most intimidating.

"Who is this *Kyra Jones* I've been hearing about?" Mr. De La Cruz folded his hands in front of him. He wasn't leaving until he had an answer.

"Mmm. *Her.*" Eden pursed her lips. As Justin's future wife, she had a natural disdain toward all of his ex-girlfriends - Kyra especially.

"So you do know her?" Mr. De La Cruz stepped forward. His tone fluctuated along with his interest.

"Sure. I've met her before. She's a friend of Justin's," Eden reverted back to her airy demeanor in order to derail his suspicions, all while trying to pick her heart up off the floor. Justin swore he would be faithful, but her father wasn't the first person to report back to her. And in this instance, she didn't even have to question who was telling the truth.

"This isn't good." He frowned. "People are starting to talk, you know!"

"So let them talk." Eden cut her eyes at him. Despite the rumors, sitting on top of the wooden entry table were two dozen roses from Justin. Delivered just days ago, the soft, red petals brushed against the tip of her nose as she breathed in their sweetness. She smiled thinking about all the things Justin did for her, just because; however, her pride was diminished by brown edges. Even though Eden knew they wouldn't last long when she got them, it still hurt to see they were dying already.

"I'm worried this *Kyra* may be interfering with our plan," her father continued. "She's become a distraction – a distraction we *don't* need," he hissed.

"Trust me, Daddy. Justin isn't going anywhere." Eden drew her confidence from the closest mirror, and still came up short. It didn't matter that she had been complimented on her looks since the day she was born. Her father's comments tickled insecurities that lay far beneath the surface. "Who told you that silly nonsense, anyway?" she asked, careful not to sound too curious.

"Don't worry who told me. Is it true?" His retort was sharp and quick.

"No! Of course, not," Eden burst out laughing, as though it were impossible. "We're fine. Everything is fine," she assured.

"Eden, don't you dare lie to me," her father growled. "If there's something going on then you need to let me know. We have come too far to mess this up now," he fussed.

"Have I ever?" Eden wasn't afraid to challenge him. Mr. De La Cruz fell silent trying to come up with something he could use as an example. When nothing came to mind, his frustration remained.

"Need I remind you how dire our situation is?" he whispered. "It is imperative that we solidify our alliance with the Hartwells. This marriage is our only hope!"

"Yes Daddy. You know I would do anything for our family." Eden took a deep breath to keep from buckling under the weight of her father's expectations. It drove her crazy listening to him talk about her marriage in terms of business. She hated to hear her marriage referred to as a contract. One of the biggest days of her life didn't have any real meaning. Love had nothing to do with it.

Nothing more than a pawn in her father's power struggle, Eden remained fiercely loyal to her bloodline. And even though Justin was the first man to test that loyalty, she and her father would be bound forever; if not by blood, then by secrets.

With an estimated net-worth of over $100 million dollars, bank statements showed Mr. De La Cruz had blown most of his fortune by the end of 2011. Blinded by his bad habits and his title as a businessman, Mr. De La Cruz blamed their current financial situation on the recession and the stock market. He didn't want to admit that it was getting harder to fund his gambling addiction now that they were running out of money. The De La Cruz family was one bad investment away from bankruptcy and no one even knew it.

Desperate to recoup some of the money he lost, Mr. De La Cruz convinced Eden that the only way they could maintain their standard of living was for her to marry Justin – and then divorce him for a hefty settlement. He made destroying another man's life sound simple in the beginning; easy almost. And it probably would have been if Eden had not fallen in love with him.

Her father first introduced them at a charity auction, and they began dating at his urging soon after. Eden was given one objective when they began their courtship, but once she got to know Justin, she discovered they were much more alike than they were different. Having grown up constantly fighting for their father's love and acceptance, it was nice to know someone else understood. For the first time in her life, she wasn't alone.

After awhile, the prospect of growing old with Justin didn't seem all that bad. And nobody could tell her they wouldn't have some cute kids. After seeing the way Quentin interacted with Angel and his daughter, Eden hoped Justin would be the same way should they have a child of their own. Like most girls, she looked forward to settling down and starting a family. The problem was that she already had a family, and she couldn't let them down.

"Just remember; this is only temporary. All you have to do is stick it out 180 days until you can file for divorce."

Her father's cheerful reminder brought forth her resentment. Eden had already told him she didn't want to let go of Justin – or her ring – and yet he was still forcing her to do both. She had a quarter million dollars resting on her finger in the form of a flawless blue diamond. Its sentimental value was worth much more, but in his mind, there was no such thing. All he saw were dollar signs.

"I need to go make a few phone calls. In the meantime, don't you so much as utter the word 'pre-nup'," Mr. De La Cruz rolled up his sleeves, leaving Eden to wonder if he was unable to see her pain or simply unwilling. "If we are able to file on grounds of adultery, we'll have an even better chance at walking away with half of everything he owns," he schemed.

"Relax, Daddy. Dominic and I have everything under control." Eden sounded confident, but like so many other things in her life, it was all for show.

"Oh, you do?" Her father laughed. "Then where is Justin? Shouldn't he have been home by now?"

Eden choked on the silence. She didn't have an answer, but then again she didn't need one. She already knew why hours went by before he would text her back. Every time she called Justin would rush her off the phone with a promise to call her back, but he never did.

"You might want to rethink that and get back to me." Mr. De La Cruz patted his pocket square.

"Don't worry. I'll handle Kyra." Eden lowered her eyes as well as her voice.

"That's my girl," Mr. De La Cruz pulled a smile from her misery. It was a rare occasion. He and his daughter had found something they could agree on.

Kyra Jones had to go.

CHAPTER 17

It was business as usual for Kyra as she hopped in her new Maserati and headed out for the day. She had gotten used to leaving her boyfriend at the house without telling him where she was going or when she would be back. After awhile, Cincere stopped asking. He rarely believed her answers anyway.

Engrossed in their affair, Kyra and Justin didn't care to limit their love-making to late nights at his condo. Their spontaneous hook-ups took place wherever and whenever time would permit. They displayed their affection whether in private or in public. It wasn't hard for anyone to guess who bought the car she was driving. Right after he gave her the keys, Justin put it on her in the backseat.

Ready to act out another one of her fantasies, Kyra developed a different kind of anxiety when she reached for her phone. The sinking realization that it was missing put her in a panic. She dumped the contents of her purse out on the passenger seat, but the most she came up with was some money, a couple crumpled up credit card receipts, and the basic girlish necessities. There was only one other place it could be.

"Shit!" Kyra cranked the wheel. She was less than a mile from the docks when she made the painful decision to turn around and go back for it. What she found when she got there, however, turned out to be much more than what she was looking for.

Kyra sat in shock as two of Cincere's friends carried their brown suede couch to a rickety pickup truck parked out front. In the short amount of time she was gone, they had loaded up the leather recliner, two side tables and the lamps she picked out.

"What the hell do you think you're doin'? Put that down!" Kyra hopped out so fast she left the door open. Both of his friends stopped and looked at her, so she knew they heard her, yet her orders went ignored.

"What is goin' on? Where is Cincere?" Too upset to wait for an answer, Kyra sought him out herself.

"Damn it, Cincere." Kyra went on to scold him after nearly falling over the tower of cardboard stacked by the door, but when she looked around, her next breath was stolen. The living room was empty. The handmade rug had been rolled up, exposing every knick in the hardwood underneath. Even the walls were bare.

What was even more shocking was that instead of trying to stop them, Cincere seemed to be helping. She caught him with a box in his hands.

"Don't you have somewhere you need to be?" Cincere greeted her like an inconvenience.

His friends were smart enough to clear out without being asked.

"Yeah, I did.... I mean I do but that can wait." Kyra dismissed her plans as unimportant. "Cincere, what the hell is goin' on? What are you doin' with all of our stuff?"

"You mean my stuff?" Cincere was quick to correct her. "It's coming with me," he announced.

"And where are you goin'?" Kyra felt her stomach turn. The screeching sound of him sealing another box was maddening.

"It doesn't matter where I'm going." Cincere's tone was as cold as a killer's, yet Kyra felt burned by his stare.

"So that's it? You were just goin' to leave and not even say anythin?" She shook her head in disbelief. The man standing in front of her looked like Cincere. He sounded like Cincere. But he wasn't the Cincere she knew.

"What's the difference? You're hardly ever here anymore. As soon as we have a fight, as soon as shit gets a little rough, you're ready to bail out. I might as well leave you before you leave me!" Cincere went from talking to yelling in a matter of seconds.

"Look, I've been doin' the best I can, Cincere. I don't know what else you want me to do," Kyra argued.

"I want you to stop lying to me! I want you to tell me the truth!"

Silence filled the room.

"But you can't can you? All that talk in the beginning about telling the truth when you can't even do it!" Cincere went about gathering the rest of his things at a furious speed.

"So you never said anythin' about movin' out! Our lease isn't up until the end of the year!" Kyra followed him to the bedroom where she discovered the bed had been stripped. All that was left was the mattress and the frame. The four dresser drawers that belonged to him were empty.

"Oh, you'll be fine. I'm sure you and Justin will figure something out." Cincere didn't even try to hold in his laughter.

"Seriously, Cincere, this is not funny! You can't just leave like this!" Kyra's voice turned mouse-like. Between her heart and her brain, she didn't know which was going to explode first.

"You know this is the last thing I ever wanted to do, but you've left me no choice," Cincere sighed when he looked at her, but it wasn't out of anger. It was to express his anguish and exhaustion over losing her. "I'm sorry, Kyra. I really wish it could've worked out between us. I really do," he whispered.

"But you could've been out. You could've been said forget it. Why didn't you? Why didn't you give up a long time ago?" Sensing Cincere was about to cry made it even harder for her to resist. Kyra closed her eyes at the slightest caress in an effort to savor their last intimate moment as a couple, and probably ever in life.

"Because I fucking love you, Kyra and I *thought* you loved me." Cincere stuffed the rest of his clothes in garbage bags.

"I do love you, Cincere, it's just . . ."

"Not as much as you love him?" Cincere shot her a scornful glare. "Go ahead. Admit it! There's no use in denying it now!"

"Look, this hasn't been easy for me either, alright? It's not like I walk around here feelin' good about this!"

"You're the one who made it this way! You didn't have to do what you did!" Cincere screamed louder, as though it were a contest.

"Cincere, you have to know I never wanted it to end like this." Kyra swallowed hard.

"I sure can't tell. Seems to me like you got everything you need," he mumbled.

"Don't get me wrong, Cincere, you're a good guy and everything…."

"Then what is it? What's changed?" He waited with baited breath.

"Me." Kyra could barely part her lips enough to speak.

"Oh, I get it. You would rather be another man's mistress than be with me?" Cincere sucked his teeth. "I mean, I know I might not be able to buy you everything you want, but you can't say I wasn't good to you. At least I never cheated!" he argued.

"Let's not make this any harder than it already is, okay, Cincere?" Kyra couldn't bear to look at him. She had been dreading this moment for a long time, and although she knew it was coming, the pain associated with their break-up turned out to be a lot worse than she thought.

"Look, Kyra, all I'm saying is, you deserve better. We both do," Cincere exhaled through his nostrils. "I know you think you love him, but one day you'll realize real love isn't one-sided. If Justin really wanted to be with you he would."

"You're right." Kyra looked down.

"Can't you see he's just using you?" Cincere questioned her through narrow eyes. "Justin is going to break your heart just like he did the last time. You know it. I know it. And when it happens again, *don't* call me," he taunted.

"I really am sorry if I hurt you, Cincere, but I can't change how I feel." Kyra held the door open for him.

"And neither can I."

With his bags in one hand, and his pride in the other, Cincere left without so much as a hug, a kiss, or a goodbye.

Seconds after she turned the lock, Kyra slid down to the floor. She thought she would be happy, but her freedom felt as empty as the room she was sitting in. It didn't take long for the tears to start. She never felt more alone than she did in that moment.

Kyra got so worked up she almost didn't hear the buzzing coming from the kitchen. Low and behold, there was her cell phone, dancing across the countertop. Had any other name other than Justin's popped up there was no way she would have answered it.

"Hey. Sorry. I got a little caught up. I'm about to leave now." Kyra cut back on her sniffling.

"Good, I'm glad I caught you before you left," Justin sighed in relief.

"Why? What's up? You want me to meet you somewhere else?" Kyra perked up enough to ask a few questions. Hearing his voice jolted her back to life however the tone he used diluted her excitement.

"I can't. It's Eden."

"*Eden?*" Kyra nearly bit his head off. She didn't care that Eden was his fiancé. Eden could be in the hospital, and that would still be no excuse.

"Yeah, apparently she made plans for us to have dinner with our parents tonight. I had no idea." Justin seemed to share Kyra's irritation. He sounded bored already.

"So try to get out of it," she demanded.

"I can't. I already tried," Justin sighed even harder.

"Then tell her you're not goin'! It's not like she can force you!"

"It won't look right if I don't go. Everybody is going to be there," he explained.

"You mean everybody except me?"

"Like I said; I'm really sorry to do this to you, but I just found out a few minutes ago myself. Why are you so upset?" Justin hid his confusion with a chuckle.

"*Because,* I *really* need to see you," Kyra carried on with her tantrum. Her heart couldn't handle another disappointment.

"Maybe we can meet up later tonight?" Justin's casual suggestion failed to cheer her up. The way he was acting, Kyra wasn't sure she even wanted to see him anymore.

"When are you goin' to tell her about us? I know you don't think I'm goin' to let you keep stringin' me along like this," she sassed.

"I'm going to tell her. I just need a little more time. . ."

Kyra rolled her eyes at the excuse.

"How much more time do you need, Justin? The wedding is a week away!" she stressed.

"So it's not like I want to be with her. I want to be with you," he claimed.

"Then what's stopping you?" Her curiosity was pure.

"Hold on. I think I hear someone coming," Justin covered the mouthpiece. "Look, I gotta go. Can we talk about this later?" he whispered.

"Whateva Justin it's really not that hard. Either you hurry up and make a decision or I'll do it for you." Kyra hung up before he could respond. Justin might have been scared to tell Eden about their affair, but she wasn't. She was tired of sitting around, waiting for him. Kyra was ready to take what she wanted - no matter the cost.

It was up to her to make the next move.

CHAPTER 18

The following afternoon Kyra made a special trip to the capital of Cockburn Town. Hailed as the historical centerpiece of the Turks and Caicos, Grand Turk was the largest island in the chain; boasting a first-class cruise center complete with a 3000-foot pier, in addition to a 19th century lighthouse, and a national museum. The town's Salt Era charm was preserved in the form of Bermudan-style buildings which had been re-opened as rustic inns or private residences. Most of the government-owned offices, banks, churches, and other commercial buildings were located downtown, where traffic was sparse - minus the horses or donkeys roaming the alleys. Traces of sand dusted the main streets.

White wrought iron framed the glass walls of the public conservatory however the central dome made it unique. Nestled in acres of meticulously kept gardens, a colorful array of flowers surrounded the old structure for as far as the eye could see. Exotic birds made their homes amongst the diverse greenery housed in each wing. Butterflies fluttered about.

A plaque outside stated that the conservatory had been built in 1822 by a wealthy salt merchant named Sir Francis Middleton. According to history, Middleton died of malaria just one month before his floral palace was to be completed, but Kyra didn't have time to read the rest of the story. She bypassed a tour and the gift shop on her way to the tea room.

Kyra stood four inches taller in a pair of patent leather red bottoms, and the knee-length Chanel piece she had on fit her better than the mannequin. Factor in her wild curls and her favorite matte lipstick, and it was her confidence that was wearing off. The last conversation she had with Justin prompted her search for reassurance. However, it soon became clear that if she expected to find it there, she came to the wrong place.

"Kyra." Eden faked a smile for appearance's sake. "Care to join me for some tea?"

"I don't like tea," Kyra went cold.

"So, I don't like you. And yet here we are." Eden tipped the teapot, perky as could be.

"Cut the bullshit, Eden. Where's Justin?" Kyra made her irritation known. Hidden behind a pair of sunglasses and a floppy sunhat, Eden still felt her dirty looks.

"He's not coming. Now, sit," Eden's smile was replaced by tight lips. She dropped two sugar cubes in her teacup, and kept stirring until they dissolved. When she was done, she rubbed her spoon against the edge, and laid it gently on the saucer. The amount of steam rising from her cup made it a tempting weapon, but it was still too hot to drink.

"This doesn't concern you, Eden. You need to mind your business," Kyra lit into her the moment her butt touched the seat. Not only had Eden tricked her into making a wasted trip, she used Justin's phone to do it.

"In your text, you said you had something important to tell him. And, well, he *is* my fiancé. So yes, I do believe that qualifies as 'my business.'" Eden folded her hands, but the look in her eyes said she was ready to flip the table. The heat between them raised the temperature in the room.

"What do you want Eden?" Kyra sighed in annoyance. Out of all the delicious pastries laid out in front of her, she wasn't even tempted to try one. For all she knew they were poisoned.

"I wanted to let you know that I know." Eden leaned half-way across the table. "I know what you're trying to do, and it's *not* going to work," she whispered.

"And what is that?" Kyra laughed louder than she should have. Several heads turned in their direction.

"Come on, Kyra. I know you don't really think I'm that stupid. I know he's not working late every night he says he is." For the first time in their conversation Eden looked at Kyra, not as though she was trying to look through her.

"Well maybe if you worried more about him than me you wouldn't have that problem," Kyra commented.

"Oh, Kyra, I would hardly consider you a 'problem,'" Eden smiled politely. "You're more of a pest."

"Does Justin know that you're here?" Kyra made use of the arm rest.

"Don't worry about Justin or what he's doing," Eden flipped. "I am not about to let you steal my husband!" she hissed.

"Uh, excuse me? Justin is *not* your husband." Kyra shot her the craziest look.

"Not *yet* anyway. . ." Eden flaunted her rock. "God, I cannot *wait* to see the look on your face when you have to call me Mrs. Hartwell!" she cackled.

"Yeah, okay. Like that'll ever happen," Kyra mumbled.

"You know, I don't think I like your attitude."

"That's okay. Your 'husband' likes it enough for the both of you." After just a few minutes with Eden, Kyra had mastered the art of insulting her with a smile. But instead of cussing her out, Eden smiled wider.

"You know, I am *really* trying to be nice right now. But you are not making it easy," she chuckled. "I just think it's so funny how you act as though you are anywhere near my level, when the only thing you and I have in common is Justin. And even that is temporary."

"So if that's the case then why don't you tell him to stop callin' me? I can't help if he still checkin' for me," Kyra gloated in return.

"Because I don't care." Eden snapped a cookie in half, took a bite, and watched the rest crumble in between her fingers. "Just because he fucked you that don't mean he loves you," she reasoned.

"And just because he tells you he loves you that doesn't mean he really does," Kyra added.

"Then you would be wise to take your own advice," Eden spat. "I mean, seriously, Kyra, where is your dignity; your self-respect? Clearly, you don't have any!"

Kyra folded her arms in defiance. "Look, I'm not goin' anywhere. So you might as well get used to me."

Eden laughed. "Kyra, sweetie, you don't want it with me. You need to learn when it's time to walk away."

"I've never been one to walk away from a fight."

"I don't have to fight for what's already mine." Eden looked her in the eye.

"Why? Are you scared? Or is it because you already know you're not going to win?" Kyra smirked.

"I've already won." Eden wiggled her ring finger.

"Then why are we here?" Kyra's smirk disappeared.

"All right, Kyra, let's cut the small talk." Eden threw her napkin down on her plate. "I don't want you coming around anymore. I find your friendship with Justin extremely inappropriate, and as his wife I am going to have to ask that you put an end to it immediately."

"So you do realize I still work for Justin, right? It's not up to you to fire me. Only he can do that," Kyra mocked her request.

"You're right," Eden nodded. "I can't fire you. Which is why I'm giving you the option to quit. You would be smart to take it."

"And what are you gonna do if I don't?" Kyra's attitude resurfaced.

"It's simple really: you agree to stop seeing Justin. And I'll agree not to tell him you slept with Dominic." Eden stuck her pinky out with each sip.

"I don't know what you're talkin' about." Kyra shut down, inside and out.

"Oh, you know," Eden giggled. "I heard all the details. I know *all* about you, girl."

"You don't know shit!" Kyra snapped. "Whateva Dominic told you is a lie!"

"Even if Dominic is lying, which I doubt, Justin has no reason not to believe me. Whereas with you. . ." Eden waved her finger back and forth. "Well. We all know you haven't always been the most forthcoming with him, now have you?"

"Okay, but what about Dominic? You really willin' to put his business out like that?" Kyra pulled the sympathy card, only to find Eden didn't have any, not even for her own brother.

"If it meant getting rid of you, then yes," Eden came at her with increased hostility. "Listen, Kyra, you might have Justin fooled, but you *don't* fool me. I see you for what you really are. You want to make it seem like you're all 'in-love' when really, you're just another gutter bitch looking for a sponsor."

Kyra opened her mouth to speak, but Eden cut her off.

"And that's fine. So long as you know it's not going to be Justin."

Eden fell back; satisfied she had gotten her point across. "However, since you seem to be a woman about her money, I have a proposition for you," she continued.

"Whateva it is, I'm not interested," Kyra grumbled.

"I'm only going to make this offer once. You might want to listen up." Eden reached inside the tan Birkin sitting next to her.

"And my answer is *still* gonna be no," Kyra declared.

"I will write you a check for twenty-five thousand dollars if you to get on a plane tonight and disappear. I can get you a one-way ticket wherever you want to go." Eden clicked the top on a pen. Her checkbook was sitting wide open. The possibilities were endless.

"Read my lips. $N - O$," Kyra slowed her speech as if Eden was hard of hearing. Meanwhile, Eden rattled off figures like an auctioneer.

"Go ahead. Name your price. Thirty thousand, forty, forty-five. . ."

"Ha! You couldn't pay me enough," Kyra snorted.

"Justin was right," Eden threw down her pen. "You are stubborn."

"Sorry, hon, but you can't put a price on love. Or, haven't you figured that out yet?" Kyra tilted her head.

"Maybe not. But I can put a price on your life!" Eden threw each item back in her purse.

"Bitch, don't get treated! It's still Chi-town all day. I will fuck you up!" Kyra bumped the table when she sat up, creating quite a noise.

"*Okay.* Don't say I didn't try," Eden exhaled in her usual dainty way. "While I wish I could stay and finish our little chat, I'm afraid I must get back to Providenciales. I wouldn't want to be late for my fitting!" Eden walked away wearing a snarky smile that irked Kyra to the bone. It bothered her that once again, she was left to pay while everyone else lived happily ever after – Justin included. And while she wanted to believe everything he said, her intuition already told her how their story was going to end.

"Ma'am, is everything all right?" One of the servers rushed to her side in seconds, but Kyra refused his handkerchief.

"Check please."

CHAPTER 19

Justin held onto his hardhat when he entered the shell of what was going to be the newest Hartwell resort, *The Lilliana*. In addition to the sound of power drills and electric saws, contractors shouted orders from every direction. Electricians weaved wires together, bringing light to each fixture. Masons laid the marble floors while carpenters sanded their carvings into the woodwork, shaping its personality.

It seemed as though their vision was finally coming to life . . . Until one of the architects came storming past him, cursing in another language. He tore his own work to shreds.

"Here are the duplicate permits you said you needed. There's a back-up on file just in case. . ." Justin added the documents to his brother's messy desk. "Whatever you said sure pissed him off," he commented.

"If he wants to quit then let him!" Quentin sent the papers flying and waited for them to settle.

Justin didn't flinch. He knew not to take his outbursts personally. Whenever Quentin was under a lot of stress, he took it out on those around him. If something wasn't done the way he wanted, everyone had to hear about it. Much like their father, Quentin had no tolerance for a mistake.

"That's like . . . the third one this month." Justin used his fingers to count.

"Our guests expect the ultimate five-star experience when they walk through those doors, and it is our job to deliver!" Quentin unrolled the blueprint to compare them against their composite sketches.

"He needs to tweak his design here, here, and here. I'm not asking for much! I mean, really!" Justin followed his finger as he pointed out a series of red markings. Quentin flicked the paper before he took it off his hands.

"I see what you're saying, but why can't we stick with the original? You're looking at another six to eight weeks worth of work if we go that route, which would set us behind," he cautioned.

"Our name is on this!" Quentin fussed. "We have standards to live up to!"

"Look, all this extra stuff is nice, but it would put us way over budget, and I'm sure our investors wouldn't be too happy about that," Justin replied.

"Then what do you suggest?" Quentin showed signs of irritation before he even heard his answer.

"I say we capitalize upon what we already have. You're just going to have to make the best of it," Justin took a deep breath. "If I were you, I would..."

"Save that thought," Quentin interjected. "I need to speak with you in private." He motioned toward his mobile office, leaving Justin no choice but to follow him.

"I'm glad you're here. I've been meaning to ask you about something. . ." Quentin hung his hardhat on his way to the kitchenette. From the outside, the trailer looked similar to those found on any construction site. But inside, it was designed to be as plush as the hotel they were building.

"Sure man, what's up?" Justin perched himself on one of the bar stools.

"What's been going on with you lately?" Quentin retrieved two water bottles from the fridge and handed one off.

"I'm not sure I know what you mean?" Justin shifted under his brother's critical stare. Even with the luxury of air conditioning, he couldn't stop sweating.

"Eden called me. Said you've been acting strange. Staying out until wee hours of the morning, sometimes not coming home until the next day." Quentin twisted the cap and took a sip.

"I told her it was probably just a case of the pre-wedding jitters." He shrugged. "Although I must admit I have my own suspicions." Quentin's eye began to twitch. "You're seeing Kyra again, aren't you?"

His question fell flat.

"Aw, shit. Here we go again." Justin cursed under his breath. He knew what Quentin was going to say before he even said it.

"Damn it, Justin! Now even I'm convinced that bitch got you whipped!" he erupted. "When are you going to leave that girl alone? Hate to say it but Dad was right," he snickered.

"Look, we're both grown. I think Kyra and I are old enough to make our own decisions," Justin noted.

"Yeah, and I'm telling you you're not making a very good one!" Quentin stopped to let his words sink in. "Think about it, Justin. What does Kyra stand to lose in all of this?" Justin avoided his stare and his questions, forcing him to jump back in and take control of the conversation.

"Exactly!" his conclusion was matter-of-fact.

"Don't worry about me. I got this. I know what I'm doing," Justin sounded confident, but there was no convincing Quentin.

"Justin, she will only continue to bring you down," he argued. "Getting shot wasn't enough for you? What will it take? I need to know!"

"You make it sound like Kyra tried to kill me herself!" Justin spoke up in her defense. "We were in the wrong place at the wrong time! No one was supposed to get hurt!"

"How do you know it wasn't a set up? Maybe it was really you who was supposed to get robbed that night?" Quentin surmised.

"No. That's not true." Justin wouldn't even entertain the thought.

"That's what you think but how do you know?" Quentin pressed.

"Because I was there," Justin chipped in. "Plus, you don't know Kyra like I do. She wouldn't do me like that."

"I wouldn't be so sure. I don't think any of us knew Kyra as well as we thought we did."

"Kyra's not this mean-spirited person y'all try to make her out to be. We talked about happened, and she feels really bad about it."

"And she should!" Quentin's eyes looked like they might pop out of his head. "She's the one who got you into that mess in the first place!"

"Fuck you, Quentin! Why are you always bringing up old shit?" Justin fumed. "That shit happened how many years ago? When are you going to let it go?"

"*Oh!* I get it! That's all it was! A big *misunderstanding*," Quentin peppered his sentence with sarcasm. "You'll believe anything she tells you, won't you?" he scoffed.

"I don't care what you say. You can't keep me from seeing her," Justin rebelled.

"I don't even see why this is such an issue for you! You should be so angry with her you shouldn't even *want* to see her!" Quentin yelled.

"Because I still love her, all right. . ." Justin met his brother eye-to-eye.

"Justin, I swear if you go back to her -"

"What are you going to do? Tell on me? Go ahead. Tell whoever you need to." Justin put his chin up causing Quentin to clench his jaw. If Justin weren't his brother, he would've punched him.

"I just don't get it, Justin. Make me understand what it is you love about Kyra oh-so-much? Doesn't it bother you that she left to be with another man?" Quentin took another swing at his pride. The hurt on Justin's face let him know his words had connected, and that his tongue caused more damage than his fists ever could.

"Whatever, I don't have to explain myself to you or anybody!" he insisted. "I know what's real and that's all that matters!"

"So you still can't explain how you almost died chasing her ass halfway across the globe after she done ran off at a moment's notice with some rude boy; some lowlife drug dealer who 'just so happened' to be her ex?"

Quentin's eyes looked like slits. "Justin! She led you right into that shit!" his anger flared. "And I hate to be the one to break it to you, but technically, you ran away. I don't know where you get off with these outrageous claims about Mom and Dad cutting you off and putting you out? They have been nothing short of supportive! We all have!"

"I did not 'run away'! I was going to come back! Matter of fact, I tried to come home! But because of them, I was stranded! Dad held my money until I was 21, while Mom sat there and let him! That makes her almost as bad as him!" Justin claimed.

"When are you going to stop trying to throw blame around here? The only person you have to blame is yourself!" Quentin put an end to his whining when he invaded his personal space. "You left when they were out of town! They come home and nobody's seen you. No one knew where you were or what happened to you. You didn't tell anyone where you were going. Not even me! The least you could've done was called and filled me in on what the fuck was going on!" he barked. "And you had the nerve to take Michael with you? You chose him to hold you down over your own brother?"

Justin threw his hands up in the air.

"I already told you Mike wasn't supposed to come! Besides, if you came instead, that would've put you in the same predicament as me. True?"

"No. Had I been there nothing would have happened!" Quentin hollered.

"And what were you going to do, Quentin? Save the day like some superhero or something? You sound stupid." Justin twisted his mouth.

"Yeah, well . . . I would've never let it come to this." Quentin's passion ran dry.

"You think I went there knowing everything was going to turn out like it did? Not really! So you can stop rubbing my mistake in my face any day now, okay? I'm sorry! Damn! How many times do I have to say it?" Justin huffed some more.

"Look, Justin, try to understand Mom and Dad don't want to see you throw your future away over some girl. Neither do I. We're just trying to protect you."

"Thanks, but I don't need you to protect me. I can take care of myself." Justin straightened his shoulders. After almost being outcast from the only world he had ever known, and practically disowned by his parents, he had grown used to facing his problems alone.

"Imagine the sensationalism if someone had gotten word of what really happened that night," Quentin went on. "The media would've torn you and Kyra apart had they heard the real story. We would've had reporters from every news network swarming the island asking for an interview."

Justin said nothing.

"Is that what you wanted? Paparazzi waiting to question you the moment you step out the door? Hiding in the bushes just to get a picture of you and your floozy little girlfriend?"

Justin grimaced. "You're right. Maybe it would've been better if I had just died in Chicago? Then you wouldn't have to worry about me or my problems!"

Quentin looked stunned. "You take that back!" he demanded.

"Why? You know it's true!"

"Justin, when we almost lost you, everything changed. . . *You* changed!" Quentin's anger was slowly rising.

"You're telling me? Dad barely even talks to me, and look at you. You've got it made!" Justin referenced their surroundings.

"Look, I know you might not see it this way, but Mom and Dad did you a favor sending you to rehab when they did. You needed more help than any of us could give. "

"They sent me away so they didn't have to deal with me," Justin corrected.

"The last thing you needed was to have complete strangers poking around in your personal affairs, following you wherever you go, dissecting your every move, every decision! Exposing every aspect of your life you had hoped to keep secret, all for the sake of a good story; for someone else's entertainment! Your life would've been on display for the whole world to see and judge."

"Oh, come on!" Justin laughed off his exaggeration, but Quentin refused to let up.

"I'm serious, Justin! Do you have any idea how that headline would have read: 'HARTWELL HEIR WOUNDED IN BOTCHED DRUG DEAL'? God only knows. You read the tabloids!"

"Why are you always so worried about what other people have to say?" Justin looked perplexed. "Who cares what they think. This is my life! I have a right to do what makes me happy!" he argued.

"This isn't about *you*, Justin! This is about all of us as a family!"

"No! No, it's not!" he sneered. "This isn't about love or family! It's about money! It's always been about money! That's all any of you care about!"

"If that's what you think, then you have yet to understand what it means to be a Hartwell, dear brother. We were born into privilege and with that come certain responsibilities. There are certain things we simply cannot do . . ." Quentin explained. "You think I don't know that?" Justin sighed. He had heard the same speech one too many times from his parents. Being born into a wealthy family was like the gift he never asked for. Growing up, it seemed like no matter how hard he tried to break free he was ultimately bound by family name and fortune. Most people would assume it would be great to spend their childhood in a mansion, but as he got older, the walls that fenced him in started to make it feel more like a prison.

Not much had changed since then. Even as a grown man, Justin still wasn't allowed to make any decisions for himself. He wasn't entitled to his opinions. He had no control over anything. It was as though his life had already been mapped out for him. He was simply going through the motions.

"Now you listen to me, Justin. This right here; is not a game. This is serious business," Quentin grit his teeth. "Our father built this company from the ground up. He's relying on us to uphold the Hartwell legacy long after he's gone. Therefore, I need to know I can trust you. I need to know you can be responsible."

"That's if he doesn't leave it all to you. It's no secret you've always been his favorite," Justin flashed his resentment.

"Whatever. The bottom line is, we still have a business to run. Not to mention, you're getting married in less than a week! *Those* are the things you need to be thinking about right now! Not some ghetto hoodrat like Kyra! If you continue to pursue her you could compromise everything you've worked for!" Quentin gripped him by the shoulder. "Look, I know you might not want to hear this, but you need to take a long look at your life, J. Seriously. I know this isn't what you want. It can't be." His eyes were filled with worry.

"I don't think I know what I want. . ." Justin's confession came in the form of a hopeless sigh. He loved Kyra and Eden each for different reasons, but the island of Prince Paul wasn't big enough for the both of them. He had to make a decision and soon.

"You know what you have to do," Quentin hinted at a solution. "Eden is a great catch. Only a fool would mess that up," he added.

"Look, even if I do break-up with Kyra now, it won't make a difference. It's not like that's going to change what I've done or how I feel," Justin stressed.

"No, but it's a start. I trust you'll do the right thing." Quentin patted him on the back for encouragement. Each had his own interpretation of the "right" decision when it came to his relationship, and they couldn't be more different.

Justin couldn't picture a future without his family *or* Kyra. And while marrying Eden would make him more valuable in the eyes of his father, that also meant Kyra would be free to marry someone else, and he didn't like that idea either. He didn't know when every glance at the calendar became so painful, but with the 13th rapidly approaching, his doubts were beginning to creep up on him. Justin made a serious commitment when he asked Eden to marry him, and being the man that he was, he felt obligated to keep it. It was too late to take it back.

"Answer me this. . ." The sound of his brother's voice stopped him in his tracks. "Is she worth it?"

Justin refused to answer him. Much like his love for her, Kyra's worth was one thing he never felt the need to question . . . Until now.

CHAPTER 20

The time was 10 PM which meant Justin was officially two hours late. The seductive click of Kyra's heels echoed throughout her newly-furnished apartment as she wandered about, wasting time. A half-empty wine bottle in one hand and her phone in the other, she could feel her frustration mounting with each minute that passed. Justin told her he was on his way over, but that was before he stopped answering her texts altogether. Even worse was the fact that her last attempt to reach him was met by, *"Your call has been forwarded to an automated voice message system..."*

Justin turned his phone off, but that didn't stop Kyra from trying to get through. She kept calling back-to-back, hoping it would ring, when a knock at the door distracted her. Kyra held her breath, almost sure she was hearing things, but the second knock was much louder, and the person on the other side much more determined to get in.

"Kyra, open the door! I know you're in there!"

Kyra hurried over to the peephole. The angry voice on the other end had a familiar face.

"Where the fuck you been?" Kyra threw her attitude at Justin first chance she got. He squeezed his way in without an apology.

"I had some stuff I needed to take care of." Justin didn't say much else, but his distress was evident. Something wasn't right.

"Yeah, well, you need to get your girl. I'm not going to have her disrespecting me." Kyra shifted her weight.

"Who?" Justin scrunched his face.

"That bitch Eden!" Kyra got loud with him. "You better watch her," she warned.

"What did she do?" Justin inquired.

"Come on now, Justin. I know you don't think I actually *wanted* to talk to her!" Kyra groaned.

"You did *what?*" Justin's anger surged.

"She hit me up from your phone. I thought it was you!" she squealed.

"When was this?" he questioned.

"Like two days ago." she said.

"And you're just now telling me?"

"I thought you knew!"

"No. I didn't." Justin's thoughts became clouded. He thought he had been careful deleting texts and erasing the call log, but it turned out he wasn't as careful as he thought. "What did she say?" he asked.

"That she knows about us," Kyra was straightforward in her reply.

"So you told her?" Justin raised his brow.

"I didn't have to. She already knew."

"I told you not to say anything!" Justin ran his hand over his face as though she had just made a major mistake.

"Shit, somebody had to!"

"Yeah, but it wasn't supposed to be you!" he argued. "Damn it, Kyra! Now what am I supposed to do?" Justin exhaled through his nostrils. Once he broke eye contact, it was damn near impossible to re-establish.

"Baby, what's the matter? I know you didn't come all this way just to argue. . ." Kyra pulled on his collar. She pressed her body against his but he didn't seem to appreciate her womanly softness.

"We need to talk." Barely able to resist her allure, Justin blocked her from the bedroom.

"Can't it wait?" Kyra looked confused as to why he would dodge her kisses. Every time she tried to touch him he removed her hands.

"No, I think its best I tell you now," Justin put his head down.

"What is it? Justin, you're scarin' me." Kyra's anxiety kicked in. Her heart felt heavy, like it could stop beating at any minute.

"I need to ask you something. And I need you to tell me the truth." Justin took a deep breath and held it.

"Of course." Kyra nodded.

Justin took his time choosing his next words. "Have you ever been to a club called Bongos?"

His question drained the oxygen from the room.

"Yeah, I went there once with Meeka. Why?" Kyra did her best to downplay the experience. Inside, she was screaming.

"That night after the club, did you leave with Dominic?" Justin squinted in suspicion.

"*No!* Why would you even ask me somethin' like that?" Kyra didn't even have to think about her answer, but Justin didn't believe her.

"Eden told me y'all slept together," he said.

"You sound ridiculous!" Her laughter was weak.

"Look me in my eyes and tell me it isn't true," Justin pleaded.

"So you're gonna take her word over mine?" Kyra deflected his questions with her own. "Seriously, Justin, do you even hear yourself right now? Think about what you're sayin'!"

"*Don't you fucking lie to me, Kyra,*" he snarled.

"Nothin' happened! I swear!" Kyra recoiled in fear. One of her deepest, darkest secrets was coming to light, and there was nothing she could do to stop it. She stuffed so many skeletons in her closet she ran out of room.

"Nothing happened? Nothing at all. . ." Justin continued to dig until he struck a confession.

"No. . ." Kyra's voice broke. One look in her eyes was all the confirmation he needed.

"You know what, Kyra? Stop. Just stop." Justin didn't want to hear anymore. He didn't care to know the details. Nothing could calm the anger in his eyes or the pain in his heart.

"What does it matter? We weren't together at the time!" Kyra reached for his arm, but Justin wouldn't let her touch him.

"Is that supposed to make me feel better?" he snorted. "God, Kyra! You think I need this shit? I have enough to worry about as it is!" he yelled.

"Whateva. *I'm* the one who should be mad! You're the one who's getting married in three days!" she screamed.

"So when were you going to tell me about you and Dominic, huh? Or were you just not going to say anything?" He shrugged.

"What don't you get, Justin? There is *nothin'* to tell! *Nothin'* happened!"

Justin shook his head.

"You know what, Kyra. I've been thinking . . . I think it's best we end this now. Before someone gets hurt. . . " he muttered.

"Wow. It's a little late for that, don't you think?"

Kyra staggered over to the closest chair and collapsed. Justin might as well have her kicked in the stomach. His betrayal hurt just as bad.

"You said we were in this together. It was supposed to be me and you 'til the end! What happened?"

Her misty eyes tried to put his facial features into focus.

"Please don't start crying. . ." his answer was gruff. "It's not that I don't still love you, Kyra. It's just . . . not the same," Justin whispered.

"How dare you sit up here and tell me you love me! You don't *love* me!" Kyra jumped up in his face, and he still wouldn't look at her.

"Yes, I do," he sighed.

"Then *why* are you still with her?" she whimpered.

"Because I love her, too."

Justin's confession had the same effect as hitting her with a Mack truck. The shock was the only thing that stopped her from crying.

"So you mean to tell me that after everything we been through, that's it? We're done?" Kyra furrowed her brow.

"I'm sorry, Kyra. I can't do this anymore." Justin dropped his shoulders.

"It's a yes or no question." Kyra clenched her eyes shut, trying to keep the tears in.

"Then I'm sorry. But . . . my answer is yes."

"Wait." Kyra pushed against him to keep him from leaving. "Are you sure you don't need more time to think about this?"

"I have."

"And you're sure this is what you want?" Kyra swallowed what little hope she had left.

"I am." A single head-nod confirmed his wishes.

"Baby, listen to me. I promise nothin' like this is ever, *ever* gonna happen again. I put that on everythin'. I only wanna be with you." Kyra pledged her devotion to him, but it didn't seem to have an effect.

"You got that right. I can't be with you if I can't trust you and I *don't* trust you, Kyra."

His stare pierced her soul. "I put everything on the line for you. I put my *life* on the line for you! And this is how you repay me?"

"Justin, I made a mistake. People make mistakes!" Kyra's sniffling broke into full fledged crocodile tears.

"And I'm done paying for them!" Justin wasn't moved.

"So that's what this is really about? You're still mad about what happened in Chicago?" Kyra wiped her eyes. The tightness in her chest made every breath that much more difficult. Her heart was working overtime to keep her alive.

"Do you know what my life has been like since then? Do you?" Justin squinted. "I'm the one who's been catching hell over that shit when I didn't even do anything!" he complained.

"So I'm the bad guy in all of this? And you're innocent?" Kyra got so worked up she got her hands involved. "From day one you've been lyin' about who you are!"

"Yeah, and apparently I'm not the only one!" Justin hollered.

"Oh, don't you think for one minute I forgot about your little affair with Veronica! No wonder she never liked me! You were probably messin' with her the whole time!"

Justin laughed.

"You're a real piece of work, you know that, Kyra? You always want to be the first one to call somebody out for lying and look at you!"

"Our entire relationship has been based on lies!" Kyra countered.

"And you see how far that has gotten us?" Justin shook his head. "Quentin was right about you. Here I thought it was my fault you ran off with that bumbaclot, but no! Turns out that was the plan all along! Hell, for all I know, it really was me who was supposed to get robbed that night!"

"Uh-uh! I swear that's not how it was!" Kyra's jaw dropped. "I wasn't even gonna go until you and li'l miss priss hooked back up!" she cried.

"Oh, please! Don't give me that shit!" Justin waved her off.

"Go ahead, Justin. Say whateva you want about me, but you just remember this *all* started with your lies! Had you kept it 100 from the beginnin', shit would've been straight. But, see, that's the problem with tellin' a lie. Once you tell one, you gotta tell another, and after so long, even you start to believe it. You start to question everythin' you thought you knew. What is right? What is wrong? Before you know it, you won't know which is which . . . I bet you don't even know what's real anymore. Do you, Justin?" Kyra fired back.

"Bullshit!" Justin looked her over in disgust. "What don't you think I know about you, Kyra? Huh? Like your shit don't stink? You think I don't know you were fucking Makai *before* I got back with Veronica? What do you think made me do it? I already told you I didn't care about her!"

Kyra stuck her tongue in her cheek. She didn't have a comeback for that one. "Yeah, you didn't know that did you? I don't hear you talking shit now!" Justin continued.

"And how was I supposed to know that? You made it seem like you moved on. I thought you didn't want me anymore." Kyra's eyes filled with tears that refused to fall.

"Whatever, Kyra, I'm done!" Justin's exasperation followed him out the door.

"Justin, wait!" Kyra chased him to the street.

"Lose my number." Justin sidestepped her pleas.

In her final act of desperation, Kyra wedged herself between him and his car, but he still managed to open the door, even with her on it. Justin was leaving, and there was nothing she could do to make him stay.

"Justin, please!" Kyra pounded on the glass, but Justin refused to roll down the window. Never-ending tears streamed down her face as she watched him drive away. Her one true love was gone. And this time, he wasn't coming back.

CHAPTER 21

"That damn, Kyra Jones!" Once back at her suite, Eden threw back her hood, revealing her identity. It was unusual to see her dressed down in jeans and flats, but Eden wasn't too good to get her hands dirty. Inside her tote bag was a fresh roll of duct tape and rope she never got to use.

"Ugh! I was *right* there! I almost had her!" Eden vented to her brother.

"What happened? You find out anything new?" Dominic put down the book he was reading in hopes she had an even better story to share.

"Not really. Justin showed up not long after I did." Eden removed a clean blade from behind her back and set it on the table in front of him.

"Where did you go?" Dominic sat up straight. His eyes stayed glued to the knife while Eden focused on making herself more comfortable.

"I took a little ride over to Colony Park."

"You went to Kyra's?" Dominic stood to engage her further.

"I had to." Eden secured her hair in a ponytail.

"What the hell, Eden? You're lucky you didn't get caught!" Dominic panicked. "Did anybody see you?" he whispered.

"It was dark. No one even knew I was there." Eden rolled her eyes hard.

"What do you think Justin was doing there so late?" Dominic's curiosity helped balance out his jealousy however the look on his face was as serious as his sister's.

"I'm not sure. He didn't stay long. The way he came storming out of there, I'm guessing they had a fight." Eden's lips curled on their own. She hated to acknowledge Justin's affair, let alone discuss the details.

"Do you know what it was about?"

Eden sighed. As if she wasn't already mad enough at Justin for foiling her plan, Dominic's questions annoyed her even more.

"I don't. But, if I had to guess, I'd say it probably had something to do with the fact that she's a stank ho who don't know when to keep her legs closed." Eden's chipper tone failed to disguise her malice. Dominic put an end to her nasty remarks with an even nastier look.

"I don't know. I was too far away to hear what they were saying." Eden knew when to wrap it up. She and her brother were already on questionable terms so it was best to leave out the part where she told Justin about his encounter with Kyra, and that most likely, the argument wasn't about her or the wedding. They were fighting over him.

"Look, Dominic, you might not always agree with the way I do things, but I told Daddy I would take care of it, and that's exactly what I plan to do - with or without your help!" she declared.

"He never said anything about killing anyone!" Dominic stepped up.

"What's the matter? You don't have it in you?" Eden argued.

"I already did my part," Dominic snapped. "Now it's time for you to do yours," he ordered.

"We can try again tomorrow. You can come with me. " Eden begged.

"Nah, it's too risky," he warned.

"I'm not about to let her get away with this, Dominic!" Eden lashed out at him as if he were to blame. "I mean, who the hell does she think she is? Fucking *my* man and then talking shit to me about it? That bitch crossed the line!"

"I know you don't like her, but I say we keep Kyra around for the time being. She might just be more useful to us alive," Dominic went on, still as calm as before.

"Yeah, maybe to you," Eden snorted. "What if she shows up on Saturday? What are we going to do then?" she asked.

"Maybe we can scare her?" he proposed.

"And how do you suppose we do that? Prank phone calls?" Eden sucked her teeth. "We're not in high school anymore, Dominic. That's not going to cut it," she said.

"You seem to have forgotten that we're in this is to *make* money. Not lose it. Neither one of us can afford to catch a case," he cautioned.

"And if she ruins our plan? I bet you'll wish we killed her then!" Eden unraveled before him.

"She doesn't know anything. We have no reason to kill her."

"At the end of the day, it's us, or her." Eden crossed her arms. "My question to you is why postpone the inevitable? Why not just get it over with?"

Dominic fell silent.

"I say we kidnap her at least until after the wedding. Just to make sure she doesn't try anything. . . " Eden trailed off trying to plot the necessary steps.

"And keep her where?" Dominic laughed at the idea. "As soon as we let her go, she'll go straight to the police," he said.

"Which is why there is only one option," Eden concluded.

"I'm not going to let you hurt her, Eden." Dominic clenched his jaw.

"Aw. You must really care about her." Eden's admiration quickly turned to disgust. "*Why*, I'll never know," she mumbled.

"We have to be careful not to upset Justin. We don't want to give him any reason not to go through with this wedding." Dominic managed to block out his sister's comments, so he didn't understand why he couldn't do the same with his feelings for Kyra. Ever since he had a taste, he craved her like his favorite food.

"If everything goes according to plan, Justin and I will be busy enjoying our honeymoon by the time anyone finds her body. *If* they find her body," Eden laughed, determined to dispose of her enemy and the evidence.

"You don't think he'll be a little upset when he finds out?" Dominic started to worry. Her excitement was sickening.

"Give me a couple of days with him. He'll get over it," Eden wore an evil smirk.

"Yeah, but as soon as she turns up missing you're going to be one of the first people the police are going to suspect. If they show up one day asking to talk to you, what are you going to tell them?" Dominic conducted his own questioning in an attempt to scare her.

"Nothing," Eden flipped her long beautiful hair. "Justin is the one with the motive. He's the one having the affair," she answered. "Besides, I'm pretty sure I'm not the only one who hates her," she grumbled.

"Look, the sooner you and Justin get married, the sooner you can get divorced. That is what you want isn't it?" His confusion came through in his expression.

"I want Kyra dead, Dominic! What don't you understand?" When Eden broke down crying, Dominic didn't console her. He was still trying to figure out what why she seemed so determined to get rid of Kyra. And then it hit him.

"Damn. I knew it!" Dominic exploded. "You fell in love with him! Even after I told you not to!" he scolded.

"Psh, I don't care about him." Eden kept her eyes on the floor.

"Why would you do that? You knew this shit wasn't going to last!" Dominic yelled at her…and himself.

"I said I don't care!" Eden screamed at him, but that didn't make her any more believable.

"Listen, do me a favor. From now on, don't do anything else without running it by me first." Dominic huffed and puffed, book in hand.

"I can't make any promises," Eden backed her statement with a mean look.

"Stick to the plan, Eden." Dominic squeezed her arm until she yelped in pain. Her glare followed him across the room, but Eden didn't move. Dominic was on his way out when she grabbed the closest thing to her and pitched it at the door. A photo of her and Justin taken the night that they met lay amongst the shards of glass, but Eden didn't bother to pick up the pieces. Similar to their relationship, the damage had been done and there was no way to fix it. She was broken like the frame.

CHAPTER 22

Kyra inhaled the smell of scented oils however the "soothing" effects from the aromatherapy failed to kick in. After being dumped by her boyfriend and her lover all within the same week, Kyra figured some time at the spa was just what she needed to get her mind right, so she invited Meeka along for a day of pampering complete with facials, full-body massages, mani-pedis, and of course, plenty of girl talk.

"What do you think?" Meeka spread her fingers apart for evaluation once they reached the sauna.

"I like that color on you! She did a really good job." Despite the compliment, Kyra's enthusiasm seemed strained. Hidden speakers played peaceful soundscapes to match the awesome images on the TV, but she was still too upset to enjoy any of it. Her heartbeat was delayed after a snapshot of a rainforest morphed into an advertisement for The Lilliana. The rendering lingered on the screen much longer than the others.

"Girl, thank you so much for treating me. This is just what I needed." Meeka poured a full ladle of water on the heated stones, causing steam to rise.

"Say that." Kyra threw her head back. "I've been beyond stressed," she groaned.

"Yeah, what's been going on with you? It's been a minute." Meeka re-adjusted the towel on her head.

"Sorry girl. Shit has been *crazy* lately." Kyra exhaled, loud and heavy. "So much has happened since the last time we talked."

"I feel like I never see you anymore. We miss you at the restaurant.

You should stop by when you're not so busy," Meeka suggested.

"I will. Maybe next week. " Kyra's smile lasted all of two seconds. She had no intention of revisiting her past.

"How's the styling gig? Do you love it or what?" Meeka asked.

"Work is fine. It's my personal life that sucks," Kyra huffed.

"What's wrong?" Meeka perched her elbows on the ledge behind her.

"Well, I don't know if you heard, but me and Cincere broke up," Kyra announced. "Or should I say he broke up with me?"

"What you mean, y'all 'broke up?" Meeka had to stop herself from laughing. She cleared her throat when Kyra didn't join.

"I came home the other day and caught him movin' out," Kyra continued.

"What do you mean you 'caught' him?" Meeka whipped around so fast her head wrap almost fell off.

"He packed up while I was gone. No warning, no nothing. He just got his stuff and left." Kyra motioned toward the door.

"Shut up!" Meeka gasped.

"I'm for real." Kyra nodded. "I had to order all new furniture and everything. You should come over once I get it all set up."

"Maybe you two need to take a break for a while? Couples do that all the time," Meeka maintained a positive outlook. "'Cause we all know it's one thing to love someone, and another to live with them," she joked.

"Actually, I'm kind of glad he was the one to do it." Kyra shrugged. "I don't agree with *how* he did it, but it took some of the pressure off me," she admitted.

"Damn, that *is* crazy! You two were so cute together!" Meeka squealed. "I always thought y'all had like, the perfect little relationship."

"Nothing's perfect," Kyra interjected.

"So . . . I take it you're still seeing Justin then?" Meeka gossiped.

"Yeah. . . Well I was. . ." Kyra hesitated.

"Good. I'm glad you came to your senses." Meeka went back to admiring her nails. "You don't need a guy like that," she said.

"Girl, you were right," Kyra released another sigh. "Justin never planned on leavin' her. He was playin' me all along. . ."

"Like I said before, *screw* Justin! That man plays too many games!" Meeka copped an attitude. Kyra smacked her lips.

"Yeah, well, I'm sure him findin' out about that night we went to Bongo's didn't help. Eden told him about me and Dominic."

"That bitch!" Meeka hit the bench.

"He's a bitch, too, as far as I'm concerned!" Kyra spouted off at the mouth. "Can you believe this motherfucker had the nerve to tell me that after *everything* we've been through he still wants to marry her?" Kyra shook her head in disbelief.

"The wedding is coming up isn't it?" Even Meeka winced at the question. She dreaded asking almost as much as she dreaded the answer.

"It's tomorrow," Kyra mumbled.

"Oh, damn," Meeka coughed.

"Yup . . . of course he waits until last night to tell me," Kyra sighed. "I'm sure Eden is somewhere laughin' about all of this."

"That is so bold! What an asshole!" Meeka went off.

"I should hate him for what he did to me, but you know what though? I don't. As messed up as it sounds, I think I'm more mad at myself. I'm the one who let it happen."

"Just be glad that it's over. I wouldn't think about it too much," Meeka piped up.

"I know, but it's hard." Kyra wiped her tears before they made it down her cheeks.

"Girl, you better stop it! You're going to make me cry!" Meeka fanned herself as if that would somehow prevent her own tears from forming. The two of them held on to each other for strength.

"*Aw, Kyra,* I hate seeing you like this." Meeka broke their hug so she could look at her. "That's why I'm telling you, as your friend, that at some point, you're going to have to realize its' okay to love someone else. And that it's okay to be loved in return. Until you're able to let go of Justin, you'll never be able to."

Kyra pretended to agree but, after everything she told her, Meeka still didn't seem to understand that it didn't matter who Kyra ended up with, someone was bound to get hurt. Kyra just never imagined it would be her.

By the time Kyra decided to head home, the sun was gone, and so was Meeka. A full moon had taken its place in the sky, but passing clouds dimmed its brilliant white light. The short walk to her car was like a scene straight from a scary movie - except her stress was the killer. After spending hours being pampered, Kyra should have been feeling relaxed and refreshed, but her paranoia prevented that. Worried someone was behind her, Kyra sped up, not realizing that her biggest threat was right in front of her all along.

"Nice ride." Eden slid down the hood of Kyra's Maserati. "Did Justin buy it for you?" She ran her finger along the shiny black surface. It was no coincidence her outfit matched.

"I don't know, Eden. Why don't you ask him?" Kyra shifted the bag on her shoulder. She didn't feel threatened by Eden in a one-on-one; it was the steel baseball bat she brought along that had her so on edge.

"I'm asking you." Eden stuck the tip in her face. The way she walked around toying with it was as though she were testing its weight.

"And what do you think you're goin' to do with that?" Kyra masked her panic with a straight face. The street she was parked on was dimly lit. No one was around to hear her scream. No one was coming to save her this time.

"I could have sworn I told you to stay away from him. But *no*, you didn't want to listen!" Eden raged on. The crazed look in her eye was even more cause for concern.

"Look, Eden, you got what you wanted. Thanks to you, Justin doesn't want anythin' to do with me. It's over. You won. Now leave me alone." Kyra tried sneaking to the driver's side, but Eden intercepted her escape.

"Since you won't go away, I guess I'll just have to *make* you go away!" Eden took the first swing. Seconds later, the side-view mirror hit the ground.

"Oh, *hell no*, you got me fucked up!" Kyra jumped back, eyes wide. Her first instinct was to grab hold of the barrel, but Eden wouldn't give it up.

"Let go!" Eden started a dirty game of tug-of-war that included pushing and pulling each other across the pavement. When Kyra stumbled backward over the curb, she hit the ground with her.

"Stupid bitch, you should've took my offer when you had the chance!" Eden pressed the metal against her throat, determined not to let her up.

"I can't . . . breathe . . ." Kyra gasped for air. Not only did Eden have her pinned by her neck, she was sitting on her stomach.

"Good!" The twisted smile on Eden's face said she was enjoying every second of her struggle. She liked to watch her squirm.

"Get *off* me!" On the verge of losing unconsciousness, Kyra landed a life-saving punch. It took all the strength she had to throw Eden off.

"Ah! My face," Eden scowled at her, still cupping her cheek. "You better hope that doesn't leave a mark!" Eden scrambled to her feet. By the time she figured out the baseball bat had rolled under the car next to them, Kyra had the engine going.

"Bitch, get out the car!" Eden planted herself by the bumper. When Kyra failed to oblige, she busted one of the headlights.

"Holy shit!" Kyra took her hands off the wheel and put them over her mouth. Eden was going in on the hood and the windshield, screaming and crying as a means of release.

"Eden, stop!" Kyra panicked as the cracks began to spread. No matter how long she held the horn, Eden refused to move. "Get out the way!" she yelled.

"Come on! Hit me bitch!" Eden urged her forward, and with her temper, Kyra didn't need to be tempted. She blacked out when her foot hit the gas.

"Shit! What am I doing?" Jarred by the impact, Kyra then threw her car in reverse, smacking one car into another. She didn't realize she clipped Eden until after she did it. By the time she came to, all she saw were red and blue lights.

"Put your hands where I can see them!" One of the policemen shouted from afar. Kyra stuck her hands out the window before stepping all the way out.

"Officer, please! You have to help me!" Eden limped toward them, fully prepared to play the victim. Kyra rolled her eyes at her manufactured tears.

"What's going on here?" The older policeman approached the

situation with skepticism.

"You two mind telling us how this all started?" His much younger, much cuter, partner surveyed the damage with his hands on his hips.

"Yes," Eden panted. "I was leaving the salon when this deranged woman tried to run me over!"

"Wasn't nobody tryin' to run you over." Kyra kept her arms folded.

"Officer, this woman has been stalking me and my fiancé for weeks. I think she is obsessed with me!" Eden hid behind the older one.

"She's lyin', officer! She's the one who started it! Look what she did to my car!" Kyra pointed to her smashed up Maserati.

"*Your* car... Look at *my* car!" A stranger scolded her from the sidewalk. "That's her, Officer! That's the girl that hit my car!"

Kyra looked up to see the sound of the crash drew a crowd from nearby businesses. An angry mob had gathered and they were all pointing the finger at her.

"Stupid girl," one lady sucked her teeth. "Look what you did!"

"Who is going to pay for this?" Someone huffed.

"Ma'am, do you mind explaining how you managed to hit four parked cars?" The younger-looking officer lifted his brow.

Kyra sighed. "It was an accident-"

"No, it wasn't! She tried to kill me!" Eden screamed.

"It was self defense. I was tryin' to get away!" Kyra explained.

"Don't listen to her officer. She's nothing more than a liar and a cheat!" Eden spit in her direction. "Look what you did to my face!" she pointed at the small cut on her fat lip.

"Shut up! You're lucky I didn't do worse!"

"Okay, ladies, enough arguing. I'm going to need to see some I.D." The older officer made a "give-me" motion. His partner was busy jotting down everything being said, while paramedics babied Eden.

"Her name is Kyra Jones, and she has a history of violence," Eden held a piece of gauze over her mouth. "As you can see, she is a danger to our society, and should be arrested immediately!" she demanded.

"*Hey,* I know you! You're Delmar's daughter. Eden, right?" The younger policeman lit up, like a love-struck schoolboy who just saw his crush.

"That would be correct," Eden flipped her hair.

"Arrest her!" A man's voice broke through the crowd. Kyra swallowed hard.

"Yeah!" Her heart sank listening to the others cheer in agreement. When both policemen turned toward her, she knew trying to run was pointless.

"Kyra Jones, you are under arrest for assault. You have the right to remain silent. Anything you say can and will be used against you in the court of law. . ."

"Hold up! You haven't even heard my side of the story!" The more Kyra resisted, the rougher they were when handling her.

"Ma'am. . ."

"But. . ."

"Ma'am!" The police slammed Kyra against the patrol car, pulled her hands behind her back, and tightened the cuffs. But before they could haul her away, Eden kissed the window she was propped against. A red lip-print stained the glass that separated them. Eden was the only who cracked a smile.

CHAPTER 23

The date was July 13th. Justin's big day had finally arrived. After months of preparation, it all came down to the formal ceremony which was set to begin in just a few minutes. The murmur of the crowd was growing. A magical mixture of love and excitement was in the air as the bridesmaids and best men took their places at the front of the church. The pastor opened the Bible when the wedding march began to play.

Everything was running smoothly. The only thing missing was the groom.

Unfortunately for Kyra, one of the best days in Justin's life just so happened to be one of her worst. The mistakes she made over the course of the past six weeks became a lot clearer once she was locked in a room with them. And, after spending 12-plus hours locked away from the rest of the world, she had become as cold as the metal bars caging her in. From the moment they put her in jail, her main focus was getting out, but getting arrested on a Friday meant she was destined to spend the weekend with nothing but her worries to keep her company. Come Monday morning, she would be lucky if she still had her sanity.

The day she found out Justin was getting married, Kyra might as well have been given a death sentence - except she would rather die than sit there and suffer. If Justin gave Eden his last name, her life would be over, so for her it was all the same. In her opinion, there was no worse punishment.

Kyra didn't even know what kind of charges she was up against, and she had yet to figure out how she was going to afford a decent lawyer.

She didn't even want to think about how much she would have to pay out in car repairs or how such a reckless incident could affect her reputation as a stylist. Exhausted and overwhelmed, she neglected to use her phone call. Not even her mother knew where she was.

Still clinging to the bars, Kyra took notice of the three tiny initials inked on her wrist. Whenever she got in trouble, she often wondered what her father would say or do had he found himself in a similar situation. She applied that question to many of life's scenarios, when sadly, she would never know. All she could do was wonder.

In the meantime, Kyra did her best to ignore the clock, but it was so quiet, she could hear the seconds pass. Eden was less than an hour away from cementing her title as Mrs. Justin Hartwell, and there she was, playing catch up from a jail cell. The half-inflated air mattress offered little support, especially when every foul smell imaginable was amplified by the heat. The sink smelled more like a toilet, and the toilet didn't flush. Flies pestered her for the flavorless food she neglected to eat, and sleep didn't come easy. Every time she closed her eyes, she saw Justin and Eden cutting the cake.

"Jones!" Kyra was startled by one of the guards.

"Huh?"

"You're free to go." The burly black man turned the key and pulled the gate back.

"But . . .?" Kyra rubbed her eyes. Her bail hadn't been set and once it was, she was sure it would be too high for her family to afford.

"You better hurry. Unless you want to stay in here," His buck-teeth caused him to breathe with his mouth open. Kyra was on her feet before he could reconsider. Happy to have her shackles off, she didn't ask questions as she breezed through processing. Kyra reclaimed her belongings and kept it moving.

Grateful for fresh air and sunlight, she looked back at the barbed wire fence, with the promise never to come back. However, the moment she spotted Justin's car, Kyra wasn't so sure. Justin looked especially sharp suited up by Valentino, leaning against the door. Her heart fluttered at the scent of his cologne, but none of that stopped her from walking right past him. He might as well have been invisible.

"Kyra . . ." Justin called out to her, but he didn't get an answer. He ran to catch up. "Kyra, get in the car. . ."

Kyra manifested her anger toward him in a solid stare.

"You're not even going to say anything?" Justin stood still.

"What do you want me to say, Justin?" Kyra transferred her weight onto one foot.

"I don't know. I just got you out of jail. A 'thank you' would be nice. . ."

"Oh, go to hell, Justin!" Kyra unleashed on him. "Thank you for what? Ruinin' my life?" she panted. "I have n*othin'* to say to you, Justin. Now go away!"

"I'm not going anywhere until you talk to me." Justin grabbed both hands with no intentions on letting go.

"Go talk to Eden. She's the one you want. She's the one who did this...crazy ass bitch!" Kyra fought to free herself. "You two deserve each other!"

"I heard you got into an accident. Are you okay?" Justin inspected her face for cuts and bruises.

"Is that what she told you?" Kyra laughed.

"Isn't that what happened?" Justin looked baffled.

"The bitch came at me with a bat, Justin. She tried to kill me." Kyra lowered her eyes and her voice.

"What? Why didn't you call me?" Justin rushed up to her, only to wind up with her hand in his face.

"Sorry. I was too busy bein' *attacked* by your crazy-ass fiancé!" Kyra remarked.

"I wish I had known about this sooner."

"Does it really matter?" Kyra jerked at the slightest touch.

"Of course it matters, Kyra. You matter to me." Justin had a tender moment. "Are you sure you're okay?" he asked.

"As well as can be expected, I guess. . . Not that you care." Kyra huffed.

"Listen, Kyra, we've both had a long night. Why don't you let me take you home?"

Kyra looked at Justin, his car, and then back at him.

"That's okay. I'll walk," she decided.

"Don't be ridiculous. Not in those heels, you not," Justin mocked her ambition. The heels she had on were not suited for walking long distances. Her ankles would be ready to give out by the time she made it down the street.

"I'm a big girl, Justin. I can take care of myself."

Kyra stomped further down the road.

"Look Kyra, I'm not goin' to pretend I don't know why you're mad. . ." Justin was slow to start.

"So then you understand why I don't want to talk to you," Kyra snapped.

"Do you really think I would have come here if I didn't care about you?"

Kyra rolled her eyes.

"You keep saying that. I'm still waitin' on you to prove it," she grumbled.

All of a sudden, Justin pulled his phone out of his pocket and threw it into the brush. It had been vibrating non-stop ever since he got there, but he didn't seem pressed to answer it.

"What time is it?"

"It's 12 o'clock." Justin slipped his hands back in his pockets.

"Oh my God, Justin, you shouldn't be here!" Kyra pushed him toward his car.

"I'm exactly where I want to be." Justin caressed her cheek.

"But everyone is probably out lookin' for you!" she stressed.

"I know." Justin responded, completely unbothered.

"And you don't care?" Kyra looked confused when he didn't move.

"Not as much as I care about you." Justin went in for a kiss, but Kyra shook off his game. His sweet talk made it hurt that much worse.

"You already made your decision, Justin." Kyra turned her cheek.

"You're right. I called off the wedding." The news spilled out his mouth so quick, Justin could hardly believe it.

"Why?" Kyra held her breath.

"I couldn't do it. The whole time I'm standing up there, hoping that when she walks down that aisle, I pull back that veil and see you. . ." His sadness came pouring him.

"Justin, you need to turn around and go back to that church!" Kyra scolded him in an effort to shut him out.

"What if I'm making a mistake? What if in a couple years me and Eden wind up getting a divorce?" he worried.

"How will you ever know you're makin' a mistake if you never take that chance? You can't keep putting your life on hold for me. You deserve to be happy and so do I."

Kyra continued on her way with her head held high.

"Listen, Kyra . . . Can I just say somethin'?" When Justin cleared his throat to speak, Kyra stopped to listen. "I know you probably don't believe me, but I've never loved anyone the way that I love you. You're still the first thing I think about when I wake up and you're last thing I think about before I go to sleep at night. It's been that way ever since I met you, and I doubt it will ever change. . . I need you, Kyra," his admission was shameless.

"Whateva," Kyra sucked her teeth.

"It's not 'whateva'. . . Will you please stop walking away from me?" Justin resorted to begging as a last resort. If they had any chance, he needed Kyra to meet him half-way.

"Go on. Say what you have to say." Kyra crossed her arms.

"Look, I thought I was doing the right thing by marrying Eden. But then I realized I already found the person I'm supposed to spend the rest of my life with." Justin struggled to get through to her. "Even after everything you and I have been through, I know in my heart you are the best for me. You are my other half," he confessed.

"Remember what you told me? Remember what you said?" Kyra brought up their last argument. His words served as daggers, and the wounds were still fresh.

"I know what I said, and I'm sorry. You know I didn't mean it." His disappointment weighed heavy on him. "I would rather have bad times with you then have good times with someone else. That's why I want you in my life forever," Justin hugged her close.

"Justin, please. Let's not do this." Kyra spun away from him, but he kept a loose grip on her hand.

"I don't want to lose you Kyra." Justin swallowed the lump in his throat.

"Well, it's too late for that." Several tears fell without Kyra's permission.

"Come on. I know you remember what we had. I want that back," he whispered.

"You can't have it back!" Kyra swat his hand.

"We can start over."

"No, we can't just start over, Justin!"

"Listen, Kyra, I know things haven't always been easy. And while I know I might not be able to make it how it used to be, I can make it better, and I will," he promised.

"Yeah, but this isn't just about Eden. It's about your family. The last thing I want to do is tear you away from them," Kyra explained.

"We've had our issues long before you ever came into the picture, baby. Trust me," Justin chuckled.

"I know you might not always get along, but at least you still have a father. I don't wanna come between that. . ."

"But Kyra you are my family." Justin got lost in her eyes. "It'll be different this time. You want it, you can have it. Say the word and it's yours," he rambled.

"Justin, you and I both know it's not that simple." Kyra shook her head.

"For me it is. Meeting you was the best thing that ever happened to me."

"Really?" Kyra smiled just a little.

"Really. . . If it weren't for you, I wouldn't be the man I am today. And for that, I not only want to thank you and tell you that I love you with all my heart, but I want to ask you one question. . ." Justin took the deepest breath he could manage. "Kyra Le'nae Jones, will you marry me?"

"Justin, I - I . . . don't know what to say." Kyra searched his eyes for an indication that he may have been joking, but she couldn't find one.

"Say yes. Say you'll marry me?" Justin waited anxiously.

"I need to sit down. I need some time to think. . ." Kyra put her hand on her head. There were so many thoughts running through her mind she couldn't concentrate on just one. She was flattered Justin would ask for her hand in marriage but their reality was much different than their fantasy. And, just because she loved him, that didn't mean she was ready to be his wife.

"You already know I can take care of you. What else is there to think about?" Justin added pressure.

"Because when I get married I want to do it for the right reasons. Marriage is supposed to be based on love and trust and commitment. It's not a quick fix."

"I know, but I do love you, Kyra. And you still love me don't you?" Justin looked like his heart would break if she said she didn't.

"I would've hoped you knew that by now." Kyra admitted her feelings, even though she didn't want to. No matter how hard she tried, Kyra could never deny her feelings for Justin. And they were too strong to bury.

"Then what other reason do we need? What other reason is there?" he asked.

"I dunno, Justin. You know this won't go over well with either of our parents, *especially* yours." Kyra's eyes got big.

"And? Who cares? It's not like they can stop us," Justin laughed like she had no reason to worry.

"Okay, Justin, you know I love you, but now you're talkin' crazy!" Kyra could feel her excitement building. Getting married was the equivalent of sticking their middle fingers up to the world; to everyone else's opinions of how they should live and who they should love.

"For real what can they say? We're both of age. Once I make you my wife, they'll have no choice but to accept you," he continued.

"You don't go gettin' married just to prove a point, Justin. Us gettin' married isn't gonna make everythin' okay," she argued.

"Yeah, but I love you, Kyra, and this time I'm not just saying it. I want to show you. Let me prove my love to you?" Justin pulled her in by her waist.

"Why are we even talkin' about this? You probably don't even have a ring," Kyra giggled.

"I was thinking something more permanent." Justin rubbed his wedding finger.

"Are you for real right now?" Kyra's shock registered on her face. Her mouth was wide open and her mind was reeling. His offer was almost too good to be true.

"Why not? We're already at the courthouse," he joked.

"Shut up!" Kyra gave him a playful shove.

"I'm serious."

"'Til death do us part?" Kyra's smirk grew into a smile.

"'Til death do us part . . ." Justin followed up by unleashing all his feelings for her in a kiss.

She shrieked when he lifted her in the air. Justin spun around in circles until she was too dizzy to stand on her own.

Caught up in a whirlwind of emotion, Kyra's perception became so distorted she didn't know what was real or what was fake. The line between her dreams and reality was so thin it almost seemed non-existent. With her eyes closed and her lips pressed against his, she was waiting to wake up at any moment.

It wasn't the first time her happiness overshadowed the consequences to the point of unimportance, but nothing else mattered as long as they had each other. From that day forward, Kyra and Justin would face their consequences together.

ABOUT THE AUTHOR

Cassandra Charisse Carter was born on February 21, 1989 in Reading, Pennsylvania, but her love for writing followed her all the way to Michigan. Inspired by a dream, Cassandra was only 14-years-old when she came up with the concept for her first novel, *Fast Life*. With the encouragement of her family and help from a literary agent, she signed a two-book contract with Kimani Tru, a young-adult imprint of Harlequin Inc., making her a published author by the age of 18. Not only is *Love, Lies & Consequences* Cassandra's first new-adult novel, it is also her first independent project.

Cassandra currently resides in Ypsilanti, MI where she's been busy promoting both titles and creating new storylines. Follow her on Twitter @CallMeMissCarta or Instagram: MissCarta2U for all the latest in reviews, interviews, giveaways, and events!

Made in the USA
Middletown, DE
11 August 2019